The Names *of* Things

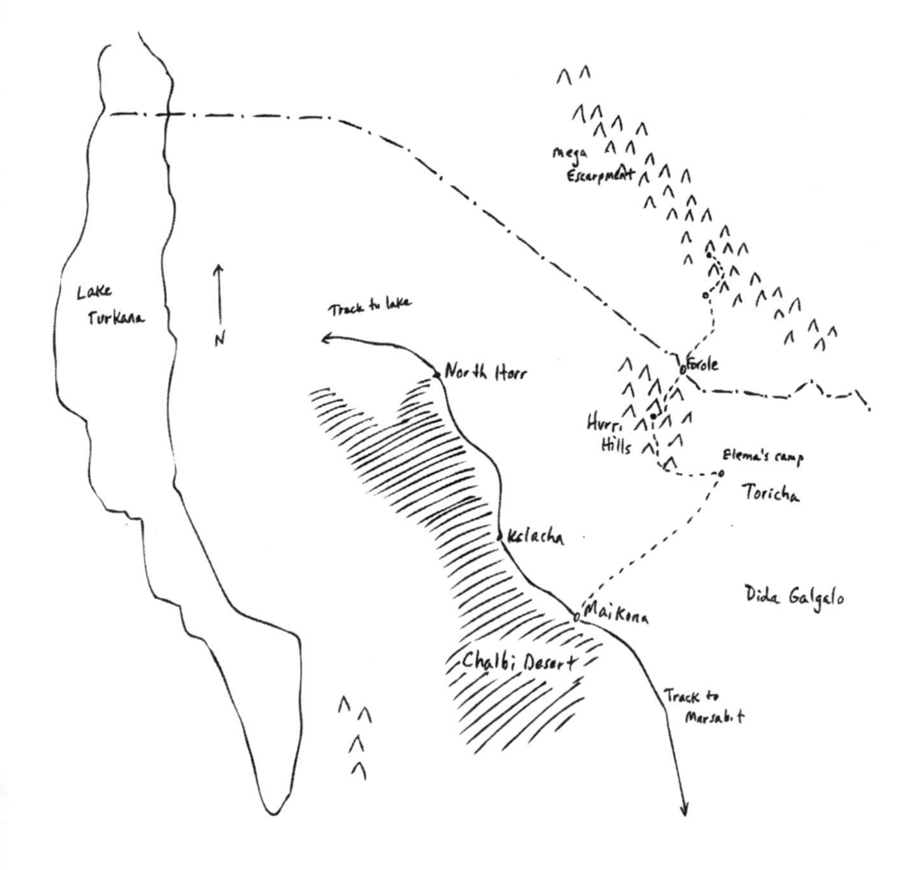

The Names *of* Things

John Colman Wood

www.AshlandCreekPress.com

The Names of Things

A novel by John Colman Wood

Published by Ashland Creek Press
www.ashlandcreekpress.com

ISBN 978-1-61822-005-9
Library of Congress Control Number: 2011937835

Printed in the United States of America on acid-free paper.
All paper products used to create this book are Sustainable Forestry Initiative (SFI) Certified Sourcing.

Cover photograph by the author.
Cover and book design by John Yunker.

For Carol

...The world, like

an old poet, gets freshened with soul water and light rising new with the sun, this

variegated, diffuse, and musical weather no one could imagine, except in sleep.

– Rumi, as translated by Coleman Barks

She hung the canvas on the wall of the studio. I'd seen her start paintings dozens of times, but for some reason—perhaps because of how things turned out—this one has stayed with me. The canvas was square, a little taller and wider than her reach. The surface was primed bluish white, thick enough to mask the texture. Despite its bulk the frame was empty, a window unto snow.

She was just as I remember her. Of course, it was before the illness, before Africa, when she was—how shall I say it?—still herself: small, athletic, moving through the room with a dancer's grace and purpose. She wore faded corduroys and one of my own castoff white shirts—loose fitting, rolled above the elbow. Her dark hair, streaked with gray, strayed from the band at her neck. Her glasses were permanently spattered with paint, so she was always alternating between looking through them and over their tops.

She'd invited me to the studio. She liked having a witness. Of course, that's me, supplying an explanation. She never said. Pleased to be invited, I never asked.

Join me?

I followed with an armful of reading. I sat at one end of an old sofa opposite the painting wall, under a reading lamp, though the general lighting from the ceiling was ample. We didn't talk. She worked. I read. Now and then I looked up to check on her progress.

She began by standing in front of the canvas. She hardly moved. I don't think she mapped out the whole painting. She mapped how she would begin, what mark would be first. But that's me again. It stands to reason. From this mark would come the next and the next and all the other marks. She took a long time getting started. Once going, she worked quickly.

Then I heard a scratch. She traced a long curve with a soft pencil from the upper left side across and down, strongest in the middle, faded at the ends. Silence. Then another, a harsh angle dropping along the left, top to bottom, followed quickly by a horizontal scrape from the vertical line clear across. Next she sketched a sort of busy, flower-like set of radiations in the midst of these lines. Not in the middle exactly. A little lower and to the right. An explosion of something. A whorl of quick, coordinated marks.

Now she was arranging and opening jars, pulling a table closer, drawing brushes from cans and drawers, assembling her kit. The room smelled of oil and thinner and soap.

I resumed reading.

I looked up when I finished the first of the articles I'd brought to the studio. There was now a concentration of color at the whorl, yellows and reds. She'd painted the long penciled curve and lines black, with a fat brush, a sort of calligraphy. A brush makes a different sound from a pencil. The pencil sounds like a fingernail drawn across the surface of a wall. The brush is like wind.

A while later she was doing something else. She'd lifted a plastic bag of white clay from a floor cabinet. She rolled a clump of it on the table. She rolled it thinner than you'd think clay could go. Pie dough came to mind. I'd never seen her do this. She pulled a long bit of white quilter's thread from a drawer, thick and useful looking, and draped it across the rolled clay, pressing it in so it would stay. She'd already laid the canvas on the floor. She smeared one side of the clay with an adhesive. Then, using her hands like spatulas, she flipped the whole of it over like a pancake atop the colorful whorl on the canvas and patted it down. The color was gone: just white and the black calligraphy. She smoothed out the clay, pressing it into the canvas, then returned it to the wall.

For the next couple of hours, she painted the whole, including the clay, with great washes of variegated darkness. She painted with house brushes, some as wide as five inches, others as narrow as half an inch. She painted from a number of various-sized cans that lay on the floor at her feet. She painted fast. She held the brushes like knives in a deadly fight, loose in her palm, wrist up, thrusting and slashing at the stiff canvas as if it were enemy or prey. The painting became a wilderness of night, the hint of ridges and plains, skyline, shadows in shadow, suggestion of moonlight.

Throughout this I continued to read, smelling the new smells of different paint, the kind from buckets rather than tubes. I could hear her breath, her foot start and stop on the floor, gulp of brush in bucket, whoosh of paint on canvas.

Late that afternoon she was still once more.

She stood as before in front of the canvas, now a nocturnal landscape, shiny with wet paint. I thought of darkest night. I thought of waking from sleep alone in bed and all that nothingness. The painting that seemed so energetic in the making now seemed breathlessly sad, and I wondered how she felt, what panic the shadows evoked for her.

Then she unclasped her arms from her chest and stepped to the canvas. She got very close and reached out her hands and traced the surface without touching it until she found the end of the quilting thread, which she pulled suddenly and with the flourish of someone uncovering a sheeted secret, and as she pulled, the soft clay ripped open with a gash that revealed the bright bloody yellow whorl beneath.

It looked as if something terrible and angry was rushing out from a tunnel. I was alarmed to see such color and movement in all that darkness. That, or there was light at the other end. I couldn't tell.

I

The present

He and the boy had been walking, save a couple of hours in the hottest part of afternoon, since the quarter moon rose at two o'clock that morning. From the settlement of Maikona on the edge of the Chalbi Desert, they skirted the Dida Galgalo plains, where you could look in every direction and not see one tree or even a bush, only lava rubble the color of rotted apples and grass between rocks, yellow as packing straw. The emptiness comforted him. The flat horizon, swept daily by unceasing wind, calmed his mind. He missed the place. He missed the people. But he also wanted the desiccation, the osmotic suck, to wipe his memories clean and blow them away.

They'd left at two o'clock in the morning because the trip at a camel's pace would take them eighteen hours, and they wanted to arrive when the camp was still awake. Two o'clock was also when the moon came up, slim as it was, and they needed its light to load the camels with jerry cans of water and their gear and to find the path amid the stones.

The owner of the camels, the boy's father, had known Abudo, knew where Abudo's camp was, and sent his son to show the way. The foreigner did not remember the boy, who would have been a child before. Now a teenager, Ali was tall, narrow, small shouldered, long legged. His almond face was handsome except for the pebbles of acne around his mouth. Ali refused his mother's help. In the end, she'd stepped in to reposition the loads and tighten the ropes. Ali made up for his lack of skill with teenage indifference. When he smiled, which in the beginning was not at all, the smile was shy and surprising.

⁂

They stopped to rest soon after daylight. So far they'd barely spoken. They sat in the shade of a low-slung tree on the edge of a *lagga*, a dry seasonal riverbed, and chewed tobacco. The camels, still loaded, browsed lazily at the branches of a nearby tree. The *ferenji* wore plain khaki shorts and a T-shirt and a canvas hat for the sun. The boy wore a black T-shirt and a *kikoi* made of Indonesian cloth with a jungle of green and blue potato-print shapes. Both wore sandals made of old tires—young people called them *Firestones*—the commonest footwear in the desert. The metal band of Ali's watch was too big for his wrist. He kept pulling it up his arm, and it kept falling down to his hand. The watch did not keep time, but it looked smart and Ali was proud of it. He sat with knees crossed and studied the plains beyond the shade.

He asked the boy how old he was.

Kudanijaa, he said. Sixteen.

Are you circumcised?

He might have asked if the boy was in school or played basketball. It was the sort of question he asked. What did Ali think of himself? Was he a boy or a man?

Ali opened the cloth, just like that, and showed him.

His penis lay like a cat against his thigh. The wound, a jagged pink ring.

The man remembered the way he and boyhood friends had shown off playground scars. It wasn't the penis that Ali revealed, or even his new status as a grown-up. It was the sign of where he'd been, what he'd been through, what awaited him. He said he was cut last Soom D'era, a good month for circumcisions.

Ali did not ask the man if he was circumcised. He asked if he was married, and then if it was the custom in his country to pay bride wealth before a marriage and how much.

The man said there was no bride wealth in his country. Then he added, in his own language, for he could not think how to say it in Ali's, that over there one paid for the marriage afterward. Ali did not follow, and the man did not repeat it. But Ali's eyes grew wide with a vision of free women. He was going to have to wait another twenty years before his father and older brother, who must marry before him, would produce the necessary camels, goats, sheep, cloth, and untold amounts of tobacco and coffee berries for the bride's family. In the end, however, Ali likened a free wife to a lover and said it was better if the groom's family paid for the bride. Then the children knew to whom they belonged. The man said he and his wife had had no children, and Ali looked at him sadly, despite his adolescence, because he knew to be sad about such things.

Nuyas, he said. Let's go.

Silence broken, Ali's talk soon outpaced the man's ill-remembered language. By afternoon they were walking again mostly in silence, smiling at each other, noting familiar kinds of tree or bush, stopping to chew and to wonder aloud how much longer.

⁂

Even before they reached Abudo's camp it was too dark to see, and he kept the path by following the camels' silhouettes against the stars. All day the windblown sand had chafed his skin. His neck and arms and calves prickled with sunburn. His feet, which had taken a beating on the rocks, ached. He walked with a sort of double limp, so as not to put full weight on either sole. He'd grown soft in his years away, unused to walking far in sandals. He'd filleted a big toe on an acacia stump first thing, and the blood made his right sandal sticky. In the gloom that evening, he stumbled and reopened the wound. He could feel the slick fresh blood. He cursed himself for coming.

Then he heard the camp noises. Faint, windblown sounds. Clatter of pots. Wooden camel bells. Tinny voices of women and children, like old songs on the radio. He smelled wood smoke and dust and the musky odors of large animals.

As he remembered it, the camp was a collection of some twenty tents, sixty or seventy people, four or five hundred camels, and thousands of sheep and goats. It was pitched now at Toricha, a place of gnarled thorn scrub below the hills of Badda Hurri, far to the north of where they'd started. He remembered Toricha from before. The sounds and smells in the night air were all familiar. But it was not the same. Nomads never camped in the same place twice. It was their business to move, to blow with the wind. Doubtless there would be people here he knew, who remembered him. There would be others he did not know. And there would be those he knew, and loved, who would be gone.

II

Ali handed him the rope and went alone amid the tents to announce their arrival and to find Abudo's brother. They planned to sleep at his tent.

He remained behind in the darkness. He could see the glow and glitter of small fires within the matted tents. Here and there the beam of an electric torch sliced across the blackness to the west, where the sheep and goats would be corralled. He was glad to have arrived, glad for once not to be walking. He was hungry and thirsty and, strangely, happy for the first time in months.

Someone approached.

Ali?

The figure chuckled. A man, not Ali.

Galchumi nagaya? said the voice, a whisper within the wind, offering the greeting of night. Have the camels returned peacefully?

Nagaya. Kesan nagaya? he replied.

It was Abudo's brother, Elema. They stood together in the darkness and exchanged the litany of greetings for evening, words you'd say to anyone: a familiar, a stranger.

Arma getani? Have you reached here?

Yagen, at'geti? he answered. We have. Have you?

Elema took the camels' rope, touched his arm, and led him around to the right of the tents. Elema made the camels lie on their haunches like sphinxes and left to get his wife to unload them. The front camel shook its head and snuffled and began, teeth clicking like dentures, to chew its cud.

Kōt. Elema told him to follow.

He followed.

At the tent door, he offered the usual greetings to those inside. They were answered. Elema's wife was working over her fire. She did not come out. Two children tumbled from the tent to see the stranger. They were not old enough to know him. Light from the fire spilled out through the curtained door. The children, boy and girl, clung to their father's legs and giggled. The father told them gruffly to bring a cow skin for the guest to lie on, which they did.

Elema sat on his stool just outside the door, wrapped in white muslin cloth, and the *ferenji* sat on the ground to Elema's right upon the stiff skin the boy brought. He wondered where Ali was. Probably drinking tea at a relative's tent. Elema's wife came out with a cup of tea, which she handed him without a word. He took it, and she went to unload the camels. As she worked she spoke to a woman in the next tent over. He listened hard. She told the woman that they had guests. She asked where the woman's daughter was and whether all the goats and sheep had been milked. Elema's wife ducked into her own tent, and soon the other woman passed without greeting and entered.

Elema was talking about rain. He did not speak of other things. The rains were overdue. The time was nearly past. He'd seen white egrets atop an acacia. Lightning flashed over the northern highlands. The animals were weak. Some were unable to make the widening journey between wells and pasture. They were dying, and the prices traders paid for goats and sheep were as low as Elema remembered.

If only it would rain, Elema said, everything would be all right.

Not everything, he thought.

But Elema probably didn't mean *everything*.

He missed details and nuances. For instance, he could not hear irony. Didn't know if they used it. He responded to what Elema and others said, echoed their verbs as they spoke, like a good listener, but without full understanding. His language wasn't good enough. Never had been. He moved through their world like a partially deaf man, reading lips, catching facts, guessing at meanings. It was only after much repetition, hearing different people in different contexts, that he put things together, piecemeal, an archaeologist assembling a broken vase from shards.

Elema did not speak of Abudo.

Elema asked the man about his home. How was his wife? Why hadn't she come with him? Had God given them children? Had he finished the book he was going to write? Did others know their suffering? Would they send help?

He answered carefully. He did not explain about her. He did not know how. What could he say? It wasn't done.

He said he'd finished the book. Only a few people would read it. Those who did might speak to others. You never know. He was doubtful. People over there hardly ever think of people here.

Elema said that was true. When our enemies are far away, we do not think of them. It is only when they attack and steal our animals that we think of them.

Elema whispered something into the tent.

They sat then for a while, chewing tobacco, listening to the sounds of the camp settling. Hushed voices within tents. The unending bleats and grunts of goats and sheep.

Another man joined them and sat on a stool beside Elema.

He did not recognize the new man, did not remember the voice.

They greeted. The man asked if he was the *ferenji* who, years ago, drew water for animals at the wells.

He smiled at the memory. He'd often drawn water, lifting bucket after bucket from the bottom of the well to the trough. It was work he could do, work he enjoyed.

He is the one, Elema said.

Elema and the man then spoke of camp matters.

He did not follow it all, something about a family's troubles, the result of drought.

They spoke in shorthand, with too much shared knowledge and too many idioms that he, after all this time, had lost or never learned.

A woman emerged from the tent with a milking bowl. She stood before him. He could not see her, only her shape against the night sky. It was not Elema's wife, who was smaller.

The woman bent down and held out the bowl.

Ho. Take this.

He accepted the bowl with both hands.

It was Ado, Abudo's wife.

He greeted. *Bartu?* he said. Are you strong?

Eh, she replied. She stood.

Nageni badada? Is there peace?

Badad'. There is.

Ijole urgoftu? he asked. Do the children smell good?

She suppressed a laugh. *Urgoftu*. They smell good.

The question was not often asked, but since he had learned it he had asked it mainly because he liked the way it sounded and he liked the meaning. Did the children smell good? Were they healthy and happy? Ado smiled whenever he asked it, and he liked to see her smile, so he had asked it every time. She lifted her hand shyly to cover her mouth.

Drink, she said and returned to the tent.

He was hungry and tired. He took a long draught of the milk. It was as good as he remembered, cool with the evening, smoke flavored from the way they preserved the containers with coals, slick on his dry throat. He knew to drink his fill and pass the bowl back. He drank half the milk and handed the bowl to Elema, who took it and held the bowl out for his wife in the tent.

The other man left. Ali turned up.

Tired from the journey, the *ferenji* lay on the skin beside Ali, wrapped himself in his sheet, and stared up at the stars, most of which were now hidden by black patches of cloud. It was eerie, like a negative picture. He could not see the clouds in the darkness but knew them because he could not see the stars they obscured. The sky was a map of the universe with blank areas, unknown territories—unknown to the mapmakers anyway, not to the inhabitants. The clouds were a good sign.

The milk bowl came out for Ali, who drank and passed it back. Ali lay down beside him on the cow skin.

⁂

Ali said the *ferenji*'s name. Said his name again. And again. He woke, grunted. Ali told him to eat. He looked up. Ali was sitting beside a bowl of meat. He could hear Elema inside the tent talking softly with his wife. He looked at his watch. It was just after one o'clock in the morning. Elema had killed a goat. He didn't want the meat. He wanted to sleep. But he sat up and reached into the bowl, feeling for a piece, and ate it. He found and ate another. He ate several more. He ate enough to be polite. Then he lay down. He cocooned his head inside the sheet. Ali looked back at him and continued eating.

Ali knew better. Eat meat when you can eat meat.

⁂

Later he woke cold, windblown, numb from the constant rubbing of air on his skin. The camp was quiet, save the ranting of goats and sheep. They never sleep, he thought. At least not all at once. He got up and hobbled over to the camel corral. His feet were sore, his back stiff. He squatted and pissed. The sky was black, no stars. The moon would have risen but no light leaked through the clouds.

He lay back on the skin. Ali was on his side, facing the tent, asleep.

It had been simple traveling. He knew what to do: Put one foot in front of the other. Now he'd come to the edge of something, and it was time to speak, but he had no words. The fear washed over him that he didn't know his lines, hadn't read the script, didn't know if there *was* a script. On the journey he'd set aside the nagging questions about what to do by telling himself that something would come to him when he arrived. Well, he was here. He'd come halfway around the world to see these people, not because they invited him, or even expected him, but because he wanted to see them, wanted them to want to see him. He wanted them to see. And he didn't want to make things worse.

He heard but did not feel the wind, and then he felt it. He smelled the dust. Then he felt drops, big musky clops.

Ali rose with his sheet pulled over his head, open at the face, and without speaking the two lifted the skins and squeezed into the tent. Before they were inside, the air was water, and he had to breathe through his mouth not to choke.

He wondered whether going into the tent was all right. The tent was not big enough for all of them. He followed Ali. Elema's wife made a noise at something Elema said. She rose and passed them with her daughter, and they left with a skin over them. She would go to Ado's tent. Ado was alone with just the young daughter.

He and Ali settled onto the wife's bed, a raised pallet of woven sticks a foot off the ground. There were other skins atop the sticks, and they lay with the skins they'd brought inside covering them like tarpaulins. The tent was designed to keep out sun, not rain. It hardly rained enough to bother making tents waterproof. Soon rain trickled through the matted roof. Rain under a tree, he thought. The skins kept them relatively dry. But it was noisy with the rain drumming on the skins. It was impossible to stretch. His cramped muscles ached from the day. He could not turn. Ali was too close.

He nearly panicked. He felt out of breath. He breathed the stale air deeply.

He counted in his own language to one thousand and then in theirs—*tōk, lama, sadi, afur...*

Slowly his thoughts dissolved into the rain.

From the monograph, based on fieldwork among Dasse pastoralists, of rituals surrounding death and dying

The camel-herding nomads of the Chalbi Desert, known to each other and their neighbors as Wara Dasse, or simply Dasse, manage the ritual affairs of death in several stages that take years to complete. But there is first the burial, awala, *which occurs quickly, usually the same day as the death.*

Most people, they say, die naturally in the night, which gives survivors plenty of daylight to dig the grave. Of course, not everyone has the foresight to die before morning. I knew one woman who died early in the afternoon. The olla, *or encampment, was pitched on hard ground that was full of boulders, and the grave was exceedingly difficult to dig. We hurried to finish before nightfall. It would have been difficult to continue the work after dark. I suspect if she had died later in the day they would have buried her first thing the next morning. As it happened, we finished at dusk.*

I never had the impression that people hurried burials because they were afraid of the body or dead soul. Dasse have a concept of ghosts, called ekera, *but do not seem to have elaborate fears of them. People told me that ghosts sometimes lurk around for several years, that one can hear their voices on the wind at night and see fires by their graves. Dasse respect ancestors but do not worship them. They have only the vaguest idea of an afterlife. When someone dies, most Dasse say simply that they have gone away. They are reluctant to talk about a dead person. They use euphemisms in place of the verb to die. They say so-and-so has gotten lost, shifted away, gone to sleep, grown old, or grown fat.*

I suspect the main reason they are quick to get the body into the ground is that the desert is hot and bodies decay quickly.

There is one legitimate reason to delay a burial. If a woman dies before her husband has handed over all of the bride price camels to her family, her body should not be buried until the husband has settled the debt. This is a powerful inducement for the husband and his family to come up with the remaining camels, before the dead woman is gone and forgotten. People told me about this rule in the context of marriage exchanges; I never heard of a woman dying before her korata *was paid.*

III

Eleven years before

He was gone most days, chatting up nomads who came to the wells, drawing water for camels, resting in shade with the old men, getting a sense of their days and nights, what they did, what they thought about. When he followed them back to their camps, he was gone for weeks on end. She remained alone at the mission, what was left of it, on the edge of the world. She and the solitary priest. The buildings had iron-sheet roofs that rattled in the wind. They were half a mile north of a settlement of thatch and wattle houses that stood nearer the wells. She filled her days reading and drawing, for she was an artist, but heat and loneliness and the banging metal roof wore on her. The priest had been out on the edge himself, alone among converts and would-be converts, separated for thirty years from friends and familiars. He was a small man with a sad livery face and a hesitant smile, wary of the claims made on his generosity. When he wasn't in his frock for mass, he wore baggy black trousers and a white shirt. He was anxious of women. Even when all three were in the same room, he rarely spoke to her, and when he did, it was through her husband.

❖

Let's go to the city, she'd said.

It was not a command. It was not a question. He said OK, though he didn't want to go. It was a way of making amends. For months they'd been disturbed by misunderstandings that erupted into arid silences.

Once, for instance, he'd returned late from a day's fieldwork.

You said you'd be home, she said.

I tried. I'm sorry. It's only an hour.

Only an hour? It's dark. I've been worried. What do you think I've been doing?

I'm sorry. I can't just walk away.

But I can wait? Is that what you're saying?

I didn't say that.

Then what?

I don't know. I'm sorry. Forget it.

What do you mean forget it?

So he'd agreed to go. A couple of weeks, he thought. He'd bring notes, write. The rest would do him good.

❖

The journey took two days. That was fast. They were lucky. If it had rained, which it hardly ever did, the lorries they rode upon would have mired in mud, and then it might have taken weeks. When it rained in the north few bothered to travel except on foot. But even in dry weather, the old machines, punished by constant use over roads as rough as riverbeds, often broke down, and you might sit there for a long while, for it was tough to find space on one midstream.

The first was a cream-colored Mercedes, big as a barge. It was loaded with goats and sheep bought from nomads at the wells. They rode with half a dozen others atop the tarpaulin-covered trapeze above the livestock. The humans were only slightly less miserable than the animals below. That leg took them without incident to Marsabit. They spent the night there and then caught a second lorry south. This one, similar to the other in make and size, carried crates of empty beer bottles, which clanked and rattled like a busy cafeteria. The thought of it tipping over and all that glass kept him awake the entire ride, which began at dawn and ended long after dark.

She covered her head with a cloth against the wind and sun and pretended to sleep.

A young man lying nearby asked if they were Germans.

No, he said, shaking his head.

You look like two Germans I met when I was in school.

Nope, he said. We're Dasse, from the desert. Can't you tell?

He smiled at this absurdity.

The other played along, switched to the desert dialect.

Gosi maan? What tribe?

Galbo, he answered.

Balbal tam? What clan?

Massa.

Maqakankenu? What's your name?

Idema. It was what children called him.

Kaenu? Your father?

Abudo. Abudo Guyo.

Abudo was a Dasse, one he'd come to regard as a friend. They were about the same age, but Abudo was as close as anyone to being his sponsor, and that was sort of like being his father. Abudo would laugh to hear the story.

The other shook his head. For a minute he simply stared and smiled. Except for the smile, he might have been about to turn away in disgust or reach over and hug him. He couldn't say.

The *ferenji* broke the spell.

I'm writing a book about Dasse.

Aiya! the other said. Why didn't you say so? I am a teacher. It is good what you do. Learn our language. It's good. It's good. Make contact.

Yes, he agreed. Make contact.

⁂

The wind and dust and growling engine soon absorbed each in his private thoughts, and they quit talking and stared out at the plains until it was dark, and then they stared into the darkness.

He was propped above the cab. He watched the headlights slice into the night. The track was rough, a pale yellow brown, banked on both sides by the void. The surface streamed by beneath, and with the weirdness of light and movement the road looked like a muddy river from the middle of a bridge. There was no other traffic. Suddenly the lights overtook a pair of hyenas, startled by the oncoming noise, and they shambled along by the side of the road. Then one panicked, turned into the lorry's path, as if to cross to the other side, and it became another of the many riffles in the road. The other peeled off into the darkness. He felt sad for the hapless one eaten by the wheels. Sad as well for its partner. Abudo wouldn't have understood his feelings.

He looked across to the teacher, who was asleep.

❖

The cooling air, soft and humid in his nostrils, was the first sign they were nearing their mountain destination. It had been night for a couple of hours. She rose in the dark. I'm cold, she said. He gave her the sweater he carried in his pack, and she curled up nearby. He noticed the dim lights of farmhouses. The temperature continued to drop as they rose in elevation. She woke again and leaned against him, and he put his arm around her shoulder and rubbed her back and tried to warm her.

The dirt highway became a paved highway, then widened into a central boulevard. They had arrived. It was late. There was hardly any traffic. Dark buildings on either side were silhouetted against stars. The grimy yellow glow of oil lamps leaked out from a couple of storefronts. On the patio of a bar men and women were drinking beer, and in their midst a solitary old man in a knit cap was dancing to the brassy rhythms from a jukebox. Nighthawks drifted along the road. The lorry blasted into the white light of a petrol station. It growled to a stop near the market. Those ending journeys dropped with their gear to the ground.

Idema! the other called down. He was continuing to the capital.

Eh?

Make contact!

Aiya. Nagayati! Peace!

Who was that? she asked.

Just a guy. We talked on the way. I forget his name. He's Dasse.

What's he mean, make contact?

I suppose he just likes getting to know people.

❖

The city was more of a town, a trading center for highland farms and ranches, end of the northern rail line, center for tourists setting off on safaris up the snow-covered mountain. The town sat on the equator. A sign said so. They woke the manager and booked a cottage at a lodge twenty minutes by foot from the market where they'd left the lorry. It was a collection of thatched *bandas* surrounded by a tall wooden stockade. The bedroom had a small fireplace and plenty of firewood for the chilly nights, and the compound was shaded against daytime sun by tall eucalyptus trees with peeling olive-colored bark and long sharp leaves that whispered in the breeze.

The cottage had a kitchen. They spent the first morning laughing, arm in arm, buying fruits and vegetables, real coffee instead of the loose tea they drank on the desert, beer in large brown bottles. He'd brought along his handheld tape recorder and she, music from home they could listen to at night while they watched the fire. He held the sack in his left hand over his shoulder. She held his right hand. They picked their way along the paths between rows of vendors who sat on boxes and stools, stacks of produce at their feet: mangoes and onions and peppers and papayas and tomatoes and cloth and metal serving bowls and charcoal stoves and loose brown tobacco and black medicinal roots and powdered orange and yellow spices.

When they found something they liked, they'd squat and greet the seller, and because nobody here knew Dasse they used a kitchen dialect of the national language.

She enjoyed bargaining with the women.

Habari, Mama? she said. She lifted an orange. *Unataka shilingi ngapi kwa machungwa nne?* How much for these?

Mzuri, Bibi, the old woman said. *Shilingi kumi.* Ten shillings.

Hapana, she answered with both the shake of her head and a smile. *Shilingi sita.* Let us have them for six.

It was the vendor's turn to shake her head.

Lete nane. Bring eight.

Sawa. All right.

They grinned at each other.

Why bargain so hard? he asked as they strolled away.

It's the custom, she said. You know that.

But they do it for money.

Money's just an excuse.

She was still smiling, half serious.

It just seems mean, he said.

Maybe, she said. But she liked talking with us. You could tell. I think it was fun for her, too. You heard how she blessed us. Besides, I bet we're still paying *wazungu* prices.

⁂

Her spirits had risen. She enjoyed the cool air, the market, the radiant, succulent, soothing green leaves on all the trees, before which a swirl of customers and vendors and produce was an exciting tableau. They strolled along the pathways, bought what they wanted, talked with people, enjoyed the change of scenery.

This is nice.

Yes, he said.

Maybe I could move here.

For a while he didn't say anything.

We'd hardly see each other. You might as well go home.

She waited.

I'm thinking about it.

Moving here?

Going home.

Her eyes filled.

I'm sorry, she said. I want to go home...I don't want to live in

Maikona anymore.

He didn't know what to say. He knew she'd been unhappy, but she'd never spoken of leaving.

Why can't you work here? she said. I'd live here.

They don't interest me.

Why not? They're people. They're interesting.

It's too late, he said. I don't have time.

Well, I don't either.

What's that mean?

That you might have considered me when you decided where you were going to work...

We've been through this.

...where both of us would be happy.

They were attracting the attention of vendors and passersby, who stopped to listen, not understanding the words but knowing the drama well enough.

We agreed, he said.

We agreed to the continent, not the desert.

He pulled her forward. She was still speaking.

I imagined something like this, where it's green and normal and people don't gawk or come out of nowhere and touch my hair.

Is it so bad?

We didn't talk about the desert.

We talked about the desert.

You talked about it. It wasn't discussed. You wanted the desert. I couldn't exactly tell you to work somewhere else. You might have asked.

You don't ask me about your paintings.

I can paint anywhere.

Then why not Maikona?

You don't understand.

I'm trying.

You just don't.

Oh, sweet.

My sister says I can stay with her.

You've talked about this with her?

We write.

Jesus. What did you say? Are you really leaving?

You're the one who left.

What's that mean?

Don't you know?

I mean, about us?

⁂

It wasn't fair. He asked anyway. He told himself he'd have done the same for her. But it wasn't true, and he knew it. He didn't think he asked too much.

I'm sorry. I hate that this is happening.

It's OK, she said. I'll cook us a nice dinner. We'll drink some beer. We'll make a fire. It'll be all right.

That's what she did with all that.

IV

Marsabit was as dusty as Maikona, but it was cooler and greener, and though nothing like the town she'd preferred in the central highlands, it was bigger, busier, more familiar than the desolate settlement on the desert. They could see each other every month or so when he came up for supplies or she made the trek down. It was a compromise. She found a middle way.

She rented a spare room at the mission with a single bed, chair, desk, wooden wardrobe, crucifix on the wall, a window overlooking a bit of grass and a tall hedge. She volunteered mornings at the hospital. She painted in the afternoon. Sometimes she joined the priests for afternoon tea. She did her own cooking. She was not a nurse, had no training. She knew enough anatomy to draw by. What she did at the hospital did not require medical knowledge. She changed beds, emptied bedpans, turned bodies, held hands, mopped vomit, comforted mothers, fetched glasses of water for sons holding vigils beside dying fathers. She sat by the beds of lonely patients, especially children, keeping her own silent vigils. She did what medical personnel had no time to do.

The nurses thought she was mad to work for nothing.

⁂

She arranged the post through the priest, who knew an administrator at the hospital. Her husband was glad she'd stayed, liked what she was doing, but took little interest, since he was off working on his own project. The hospital was understaffed, desperately in need of help, especially if it didn't cost money. It was, however, a public institution with layers of rules, largely for the protection of patients—rules that did not anticipate the efforts of an expatriate painter with time on her hands. If not for the priest, who hinted that she was from a nongovernmental organization that was thinking of moving its office to Marsabit, the administration would never have permitted a foreigner like her to arrive each day, don the frayed and iodine-stained hospital clothing, and patrol the wards looking for things to do.

She was not interested in people—not, anyway, in the manner of Florence Nightingale. She was not cold or indifferent. Just a solitary. She painted alone. She preferred being alone, giving rough form to two-dimensional planes. As long as she could draw and paint she'd have been content to spend her days in silence, not talking to anyone. She painted people, faces and bodies. She had an interest in people, humanity, the human condition. She was aware of her own humanity, and while she avoided interacting with others in her personal life, which made her seem aloof, even arrogant, she studied them, watched their faces and bodies, collected insights about how they were feeling and what they were thinking. She read moods, doubts, joys, and gladnesses, not just in the ordinary lines of smiles and frowns but also in the way a woman's neck flushed at the news of her child's achievement, the way a man relaxed his fingers when a stranger revealed himself to be the friend of a friend, how a child wobbled a foot on a toe's axis when waiting contentedly for a sibling to come play. If a smile was discourse, then the bend of a body or the tilt of a head was commentary that she studied with the interest of an ethnographer.

One might wonder why she could not have done this on the desert. The heat bothered her, of course. Other things being equal, she would have endured that. She'd spent her youth pursuing rougher experiences in more dangerous environments than Maikona offered. It was just that for once, in Maikona, *she* was the object of observation. There was no public arena in which she could watch and look and study. Moreover, the nomads had had too little contact with *ferenji* like her, especially women, not to be riveted by the color of her skin, the texture of her hair. And being a woman she did not inspire the fear and respect he enjoyed simply being a large adult male. She found it impossible to observe people who were otherwise captivated observing her.

The town on the mountain was different. It was, by the standards of the capital, remote. But it offered a sort of provincial cosmopolitanism. This was partly the result of the presence of missionaries and aid workers from down country and beyond who used Marsabit as a base of operations across the northern frontier. But it was mainly due to the presence of thousands of people from at least a dozen ethnic groups. They'd come for many reasons: they were sick, they were enterprising, they wanted to go to school or to see relatives in school, they were too poor to live back home, they thought they'd give it a chance, they had lost family and friends and livestock to enemy raids, they got into business selling livestock, they worked for missions, schools, NGOs, or governments. They came for the same reasons rural people have always had for moving to cities.

Everyone felt a little strange, different from the others. None was alone in her difference. It should be said that all these differences gave nearly everyone a certain edginess, a tincture of mistrust that caused them to avert their eyes, to move without the usual confidence of low-country nomads, to retreat into house or hovel at darkness, to own weapons such as guns or pangas and keep dogs. If they were among the very few with means, they hired a watchman. Unlike other cosmopolitan towns on this and other continents, where different sorts of people gathered at parties and enjoyed contact with one another, ethnicities in Marsabit kept their own company. They intermingled as strangers on the street and in the marketplace. No one paid particular attention to the artist.

⁂

The nurses scolded her on the first day.

You are getting in the way, one said.

What can I do?

Just sit. We'll call if we need you.

But there was no routine for calling someone like her, and they didn't.

After an hour sitting, watching, she noticed a girl in a bed set a little off from the others. She lay there, not sleeping, eyes open, looking into the distance at nothing. The girl didn't move.

She watched her. She noted the ashen, almost blurry color of the girl's skin, the lay of her body, the way one knobby knee jutted in front of her, the way the sheet fell like a tent across her bony hip, the slackness of her mouth and jaw and the vacancy suggested in her eyes. The nurses avoided her, but then the nurses were so few they seemed to avoid all of the patients.

After watching the girl for some time she scooted her chair to the bed, the far side, so she'd be less in the way, and sat. The girl did not turn. They remained like that until she left for the day.

That afternoon, in the yard at the mission, her drawing journal on her lap, she drew the girl from memory. She drew the girl in bed. She drew the girl walking on one of Marsabit's dirty lanes. She drew the girl seated on a three-legged kitchen stool. She drew the girl standing, erect, at attention.

The next day she sat beside the girl again. After about an hour, the nurse who asked her to get out of the way the day before suggested that, if she wanted, she could empty bedpans and sweep under beds.

She performed these tasks and returned to the girl's bedside. The girl still did not look at her.

She watched. That afternoon, she drew the ward, again from memory: the bank of steel-framed cots that sat against the wall with small windows above. The beds reminded her of starting slots for horses at a racetrack, lined up, ready to go. She drew the ward filled with patients. She drew the ward empty, except for the girl in the one bed off to the side.

On the third day the girl smiled when she arrived.

They never talked. She wasn't even sure what language the girl spoke, and she didn't ask the nurses what the girl was in the hospital for.

She took the weekend off.

When she returned the bed was empty. Perhaps the girl had gone home. She swept the floor and turned the mattress on the empty bed, which was filled again within the hour. Just before she left for the day she asked what had happened to the girl.

She went to sleep.

She went to sleep?

Yes, she is resting now.

Over weeks like that she sketched a life. She enjoyed the routine, the order of her day, helping at the hospital in the morning, drawing and eventually painting again in the afternoon. Most of all she enjoyed how familiar she had become and how that familiarity gave her not the company so many others would have wanted but the privacy she sought. She was not anonymous. People on the street and at the hospital knew her, knew more about her than she thought they knew, knew her relationship to the man who spent his time away from her on the desert. They knew her well enough to ignore her. That was what she most enjoyed.

She graduated in her responsibilities. Eventually she was available for odd tasks, like holding a tray of instruments or carrying glass jars and tubes from the sterilizer to the storage benches and shelves.

One day she dropped a box of jars. She'd been thinking just then how crude some of the tools of the hospital were. She was carrying jars in a cardboard box and her fingers felt the flimsy cardboard and just then the box opened at the bottom, like the hatch of an old bomber, and several of the jars dropped out and smashed on the smooth concrete floor. The nurse frowned and looked toward the cleaning closet where the brooms and mops were stored.

She set the box down and began to pick up the pieces and place them in her other hand. She was left-handed and she put the larger pieces in her right hand. She heard footsteps and, without thinking, tightened her hand a little, anticipating the head nurse, the one who told her to sit the first day, and a shard of glass cut her finger, just slightly, but enough to make her set the glass down and go to the washroom and then to get a bandage.

By the time she returned, another nurse had cleaned up the glass. The charge nurse frowned.

Someone might have been cut.

I'm sorry. I was cut. See. I went to get a bandage.

Next time be more careful.

That was it. No more was said. She continued her duties, such as they were, left the hospital at noon, stopping at the kiosk outside to buy a packet of peanuts, which were wrapped in a cone made from an old newspaper. She walked to her room at the mission, made tea and ate a sandwich with tomatoes and avocados bought the afternoon before in the market, and decided instead of drawing to take a walk up the dirt road into the forest beyond the town. There were wild animals in the forest, but it was not particularly dangerous. The elephants, most dangerous of all, were usually far away. In the daytime it was thought to be safe. People from town went to and from the forest to take livestock to wells and collect firewood.

She passed a troop of baboons foraging in a meadow at a fork in the road. The warm air smelled of trail dust and forest leaves. The road to the left, a path really, led down the side of a ridge to deep wells in the ravine. The track to the right led to the top of the mountain where the government maintained a radio tower. She took that road, though she would not go to the top. She wanted to reach the crest of a ridge just ahead, where another meadow gave a view west, down the mountain to the Chalbi Desert. From there she could see the plains, and while she could not see Maikona, she knew it was out there, and that he was there, somewhere, working.

She heard a scream and thought at first it was the baboons, and knew just as quickly that it was not, that it was the cry of a woman. She looked up. Another woman stumbled into the path ahead, saw her and called.

Kuja! Come!

She ran. The woman led her off to the right, down a slope of grass and brush, to a fallen tree, where they found another woman, lying on the ground with an ax wound in her leg. She had obviously slipped while chopping a branch from the tree, and the ax had cut a deep gash into the meat of her calf. It was not in itself life threatening, the artist knew, but the woman was losing blood.

She did not think. She did what she'd seen doctors and nurses do at the hospital, what she remembered her teachers describing all the way back in elementary school. She dropped to her knees, pulled the scarf from her hair, and used it and her hands to stop the bleeding. She told the other woman to get help. The scarf was quickly saturated. The blood leaked through her fingers, but in time it slowed. The blood thickened into a sort of pudding, and the flow stopped. She held her hands on the wound, afraid to take them off, and spoke to the injured woman in a language the woman clearly did not understand, though she understood its tone and relaxed.

She lost track of time. Later she decided that it could not have been more than twenty or thirty minutes before the other woman returned with some men, the injured woman's brothers. They did not have a first-aid kit, but they did have a cloth that they exchanged for her hands. They tied this around the woman's leg, lifted her in their arms, and carried her down the mountain.

That was how they explained things later. The cut from the jar, the blood from the woman's leg. You seized a bit of life, and life damaged you. It was years before they recalled the day's events and put them together. It must have been that way.

AFTER A DEATH, *messengers are sent to nearby camps to inform others and recruit help in digging the grave. Messengers should not enter other camps but stand at a distance and shout the news. The practice echoes another from a different but related context. When a Dasse child is born, the father sends a messenger, even goes himself, with a hollow cow's horn full of tobacco, to other households in his encampment as well as to other camps to share the tobacco and spread the news of the birth. In these cases he may enter other camps with the news. But he should not cross a* lagga. *A* lagga *is a riverbed, which in this part of the world is usually dry, full of water in the hours or days following a rare heavy rain. These meandering gullies impose natural, many-fingered boundaries on the landscape. If an encampment lies beyond a* lagga *but within hearing distance, the messenger should stand on the near shore and shout the news across. I know of no other context in which limits are set on how far messengers may travel.*

V

The present

He sat in the shade of a solitary acacia west of Elema's camp and looked out over the hot, windblown land. Though water stood in shallow pools on the plain and in a *lagga* he was told lay less than a mile east of camp, it hardly looked as though it had rained at all. The land was rock-strewn, lunar, littered with dry, leafless brush. Here and there stood a scrawny wind-twisted tree, a scarecrow in a desiccated field. The afternoon air shimmered with heat. A cyclone, the tight curl of a woman's long lock of hair, rose a thousand feet and whipped the horizon, throwing dry brush and pebbles in its wake. He watched it disappear into sky the color of a naked lightbulb.

He sat and waited, suspended in an invisible bell jar of grief.

Even here he was elsewhere. He was always elsewhere.

Today he was daydreaming about cool wet elsewheres.

He thought of watercress that grew along a cold mountain river that he and his wife had paddled with kayaks years ago. He thought of the breath of air-conditioning in a car on a blistering day. He thought of summer afternoons on a shaded porch, after a shower, a tall glass clouded with sweat, a fan turning slowly, ticking, everything clean, orderly, familiar. He thought of an illicit swim.

He'd been hiking in woods in an old part of the city. The forest was part of an abandoned estate. He had walked in the forest often but always before had stayed away from the big house. The thought of watchman or owner held him back. The house was tall and white, columned, with wide high-ceilinged porches on three sides. He was amazed there was so much land left to vine and ruin so close to the city center. The property must have been worth a fortune. The house was made of white clapboards, warped and stained at the corners. The roof was gray slate. The windows on the first floor were boarded with plywood, but those on the second and in the third-floor attic gables gaped black and unblinking.

One day he drew close to the house. He'd never seen anyone, not another hiker, not anyone who looked like owner or caretaker or watchman. He was curious to see what life must have been like at such a big place. He mounted the porch, tried the doors. He walked the circumference, looking for a way to climb a lattice or banister to see inside one of the open windows. He started a rabbit from the thick grass. A dove on the edge of the forest sounded a metronomic note over and over, clear and sonorous as a timpani. White butterflies with pale scalloped wings sniffed at tiny flowers in the grass. A lizard crawled on the peeling wall.

He found a swimming pool behind the house. The tile deck was cracked in places by weeds, but it appeared to be clean and swept. He was surprised to find the pool full of water. Algae stained the sides, but the water was clear, like water in a deep tidal pool. He was hot from walking in the sticky summer afternoon. The sky was overcast. The sun beyond was bright and glary, and it lit and warmed the water. Leaves from trees in the yard floated on the surface. Some had sunk and hung like elements of a mobile. He looked around, confirmed he was alone, stripped off his clothes, and jumped in, feet first. His body set the water and leaves in motion. He stroked across and back and then stopped in the middle and looked up at the house. He let the air out of his lungs and felt his body sink down amid the leaves and the water, and for the moment he was part of the mobile. He held what was left of his breath and wished he could hold it longer and stay there, suspended in the cool water, regarding the dark, sun-spackled leaves.

He remembered the scene now as he sat under the thorn tree and listened to the hot wind in the branches above.

⁂

Each morning the sheep and goats went en masse to pasture, and then, about an hour later, after they, too, were milked, the camels left with older boys. It was a great to-do. The small stock streamed out of the thorn-branch pens, and, though many, they moved as fish in school, the hooves together making the patter of rainfall across the pebbles. They were gone before you knew it. Not so the camels, which were loud and impatient. The huge animals stood in their corrals anticipating pasture. They faced the same direction, groaning and snuffling and snaking their tawny heads at one another, as if to argue over the exact moment the humans would come and let them out. When their herdsman finally came, the camels, like passengers at an airport gate, edged forward, jostling for an advantage that evaporated as soon as they were on the other side. As one corral left, long necks ticking forward like metronomes, the camels in other corrals groaned the louder, envious, worried that they would be left behind. The young men in charge would beat them back with sticks so they'd come out of their gates in order and not all at once. They moaned together like a colony of seals.

Only when the last corral was empty did the noise subside and the collective herds settle into a measured stroll stretching over more than a hundred yards, and all he heard were a thousand padded feet crunching the coarse, stony ground, and when that faded all he heard was the wind.

With water nearby women had no need to load camels with containers and travel to the distant wells. In dry times, such journeys could take several days, depending on the distance, the round trip twice what he and Ali had done less than a week before—and he was still recovering. Now women fetched water on foot, each carrying a jerry can to a shallow pond and returning with the full can sloshing on her back. They went in groups, as they did to collect firewood, and sang as they walked. The subject of the songs shifted from children to lovers as they gained distance from the husbands in camp.

While women fetched water, older men gathered in the shade of a tree or beside a friend's tent. They sat on stools or rocks or on the bare ground. They whittled at blocks of wood from which they fashioned camel bells or stools or water jars. The bells, some as big as gallon jugs, made a resonant tonkling sound that carried far, especially at night. A large one was worth the price of a full-grown camel.

In the shade, a clutch of men huddled around a *sadeka* board. The game was played with seeds or pebbles on a board about a yard long and half a foot wide. Into the board were carved two parallel rows of cups, twelve to a row. A player picked up all the stones in one of the cups on his side of the board—the selection of which cup to play was the trick—and played the stones out, one to a cup, until he had no more stones. If the last stone fell into a full cup, he collected those stones and played them out, and kept this up until the last stone fell into an empty cup. The player moved stones counterclockwise, to the right along his side, to the left on his opponent's. If the last stone landed in an empty cup on his own side he captured any stones in the paired cup on the opponent's side and removed them from play.

He knew the simple rules but had no head for the game, which was fast and complex. He seldom even knew who had won a round, for they could see the win coming and, like break-time card players on a factory floor, folded their cards in advance. Still he enjoyed watching.

The stones circulated around and around the board, so no one really owned any of them, and, strictly speaking, the winner was not the one who captured the most stones but the last one with pieces left to play. The game required strategy and timing, for stones on the other side would come around eventually, unless one ran out first.

Men seldom played alone, one on one. Rather, three or four others would attach themselves to each player, ostensibly to offer support but often to take over. They held one another's bodies with an intimacy and closeness he both envied and found mystifying, one draping an arm across the shoulders of another who held the folded leg of a third who leaned on the back of a fourth. They were as alert and comfortable as puppies.

Other men, not involved in the game, lay on skins nearby, cocooned in white cloths stained from dust the color of camels, sleeping or listening or thinking.

Beneath the shade men conducted community business. If there was a dispute, a conflict between brothers, say, or between in-laws over the payment of bride wealth, here it was settled. If there was a decision, such as when and where to move camp, here the men talked it out. When someone was harmed by another, here the men made inquiries, discussed, and judged the case. In this place they spent much of the day.

Fathers rose now and then to walk into the bush to check on children who were looking after the kids and lambs or camel calves. The children had an impressive capacity to keep up with their charges and play at the same time. The small stock possessed less of the will to stay with the group than their elders. They wandered. The boys who followed them included the challenge of rounding them up into their hunting sports, for much of their day was spent stalking lizards and spiders and birds with bows and arrows they'd fashioned from sticks they cut in the bush. Their older brothers and sisters ranged farther with the older, larger stock and occupied themselves with older, larger pursuits.

Days passed. He did not count them. He watched the camp from the shade. He watched the *sadeka* players. He chewed tobacco. He listened. He saw the sky over the plain turn from clear and blue in the warm morning, with radiant bee-eaters, like tiny peacocks, flashing in the bushes, to the withering whiteness and mirages of afternoon, when buzzards alone moved effortlessly on the rising thermals.

The sky held fewer and fewer clouds, and he wondered whether the rains, which had lasted the one night only, were over. He was unsure what to do. Perhaps he should go. The ground was hard enough again to travel. But he didn't want to leave. He liked it here. He enjoyed the pace of life in camp. It was familiar. If he left, he would travel across Badda Hurri as far west as Balessa, to get water, and then south along Lagga Balal, visiting camps and seeing the country through to North Horr. He wanted to visit the priest, their friend. From there he'd follow the Chalbi rim east to Maikona. He would not come to Toricha again. He would see no more of Ado or Elema or the others. He was reading the paperback novels he'd brought at a pace that would finish them before he finished the need of them. He wasn't taking notes. He'd ceased being interested in people in an academic sense. He wanted to stay with them, stay near. He wasn't doing research. He wasn't sure what he was doing.

He was grieving.

He knew he was grieving.

What surprised him was he didn't know how.

THERE IS A *strict division of labor at a Dasse burial: Men dig the grave, lower the body, fill the grave, cover it; women prepare the body and cook food for the men to eat afterward. Men say women are too emotional to prepare the grave. If they helped, one man said, they would do more crying than digging. Women are not even supposed to come near. You wonder, if women are so emotional, how they manage the intimacies of the body itself.*

VI

Four years before

She returned from the doctor's office late in the afternoon and went straight to her basement studio. She did not call into the house from the door, as was her habit. She did not respond to his greeting from the study off the front hall where he was reading in the warm glow of a single lamp. Perhaps she didn't hear him. He heard the door open and close, the flop of a coat and purse on the couch, though she usually put these in a back closet.

He listened as she walked across the living room, through the hall to the basement door, down the steps. It was not an angry walk. It was not a hesitant walk. The only thing unusual about her return was that she did not seek him out, speak to him. He heard, or thought he heard, purpose and direction in her step, and he wondered what that could mean.

He thought the worst.

This was six years after they returned from the desert.

He finished the article he was reading. He got up and went to the kitchen to fix himself tea.

While the water heated, he straightened the newspapers that were scattered on the breakfast counter.

He found a sponge by the sink, wet it, and wiped the blush of newspaper ink from the counter tiles. He noticed a coffee stain, left from breakfast, and wiped that, too.

When the water was about to boil, he called down the stairs to see if she wanted any.

No, thanks, she said.

She did not greet him then either.

He made a cup of tea for himself.

He started back to his study, paused in the bedroom, and returned to the kitchen.

He looked through the mail. He sorted bills and personal letters from junk, threw the junk away, put the bills in a bowl on the desk where they stored the bills, and put personal letters on the counter to open later, while they prepared supper.

There was a card from her sister, and he thought she'd like that, so he put it on top of the pile.

She had been abnormally tired. There were other symptoms: fever, aches, sores in odd places. She'd chalked them all off to stress surrounding a show she was finishing, a great number of large paintings.

Several times he'd come home from work to find her already in bed. She did not feel like eating.

After a day or so she would improve, return to work, health seemingly recovered. But the symptoms returned, and finally she made an appointment to see the doctor, who looked her over, listened to her detailed description of symptoms, and ordered a battery of tests. Today she'd gone for the results.

It was getting late. He looked into the dusk from the kitchen window and saw that it was snowing. Big flakes fell slowly across the yellow glow of a backyard light. The snow was gentle and silent, and it quieted his spirits. He filled a pot with water to boil for pasta and rummaged in the refrigerator for onion, garlic, mushrooms, a jar of capers. From cabinets he pulled a couple of cans of tomatoes, a tin of anchovies, an unopened jar of olives. He peeled the onion, sliced it in half, then sliced each hemisphere five or six times one way, turned it and sliced the slices as many times the other. He peeled four large garlic cloves, crushed them with the flat of the knife, and minced the garlic. He sautéed onion and garlic in olive oil, added anchovies and stirred until they dissolved in the onion and oil, added the mushrooms, spices, crushed pepper, capers, olives, and finally tomatoes. He stirred the sauce until it simmered, turned down the heat, and covered the pan. He turned the heat to low under the nearly boiling water.

He looked again into the backyard and saw that the snow was still falling.

He thought the smell of cooking would have brought her up, but it hadn't.

He decided, while he waited, to watch the snow. He got his coat from the closet, pulled on an old wool cap and a pair of leather gloves, and stepped out the front door. He stood on the porch for several minutes. The sky was black. The snow, invisible above the street lamps, appeared as if by magic as it fell into the wide cones of light. The snow fell as if part of a great march earthward. There was concordance in the collectivity. Yet each flake managed to make a separate journey. He wondered at their apparent freedom. The crystals, lighter than feathers, fell inexorably down, but the slightest breath carried the flakes back up for a moment, pitched them to the side, and they seemed to meander. They seemed to play, to enjoy themselves, almost as if they had some volition, some agency, some will to make the most of the journey. But not much. Eventually, light as they were, they could not overcome gravity. The snow was beginning to accumulate on grass and sidewalk.

He stepped quietly around the side of the house, along the steep driveway, and stood where he could see into the basement, which, given the lay of the land, was mostly above ground. From here he could look into the studio. He could see her clearly there, despite the falling snow. A bank of fluorescent lights lit the room. The high opposite wall was white and filled with three large canvasses in various states of paint. The forms were abstract. The colors, vivid and bright.

She stood before all three paintings, back to window, arms folded in front, a long brush in her left hand extending out from the right side, like a fly whisk. She wore a heavy wool sweater and a pair of brown denim trousers. They were not her painting clothes. Her brown hair, streaked with gray, was pulled into a ponytail, which curled in the collar of the sweater. He could not see her face, not all of it. The angle allowed him to see only a slice of her jaw, a single, curving line, interrupted by wisps that strayed from the bundle of hair at her neck. She stood and looked at her paintings while he stood in the falling nighttime snow and looked in at her. Perhaps a neighbor, watching the snow, noticed him and wondered what he was doing standing there in the dark.

He felt a cringe of guilt for invading her privacy, peering like that into her life. If it were not his home, he would have been guilty of a crime. Perhaps he *was* guilty of a crime. His intentions were not criminal or malicious. He felt only tenderness and remorse. He sighed deeply. He tried to imagine what she was feeling. The wandering snowflakes moved him to wonder what this moment would have been like had they never gone away, had their lives been different. What would she be thinking now? What would she feel? What would he?

She returns from a day of painting and teaching. She is happy to be home and tired. It is cold outside, snowing, so she makes a fire. A while later I come in from a walk. She greets me as I enter, banging snow from the sides of my boots. We embrace. Perhaps she warms my cheeks with her hands. We are giddy with the welcome of each other. We cook a meal together, she chopping onions, me mashing garlic and filling the pasta pot with water. We eat by candlelight, talk of ordinary things—a child who sets out to draw a butterfly and finds a forest, another whose auburn hair spills into a jar of red paint, but instead of being annoyed the girl and her teacher think it is funny. I have spent the day reading and now find the book and passage and read aloud to her something that has moved me and that moves her. We nod and smile, easy in each other's eyes. Afterward we tumble into bed without bothering about the dishes, and our lovemaking is fresh and new and like before, and that is as it has been but not so light, so free, for we are actually falling more surely and quickly.

He stood in the snow, tried to imagine what she was feeling, and came up empty. He did not know enough. She was perfectly still, standing there, more model than painter. The cold made him fidget, and several times as he stood watching he shifted his weight from leg to leg. She did not shift, not once. She was a statue.

NOMADS PLACE GRAVES *beside but just outside their camps, men to the east, beyond the camel corrals, women to the west, beyond the pens of sheep and goats. I have heard about but not seen men being buried inside their camel corral. Graves for infants are dug in the tent, beneath the hearth.*

VII

The next year, another winter. The illness had advanced. The snow began quietly with flakes so big they reminded him of handkerchiefs. The flakes grew heavy as the day turned and no longer took their time on the way to the ground. As the snow accelerated a wind picked up, and the resulting blizzard made the air white with a fog of swirling snow. The storm threatened to cancel the gallery opening, but by dark the wind had quit and the snow fell as it had in the morning—quiet, benign, like snow in one of those shaken glass paperweights with a winter scene inside.

They stood alone together at the window of the second-story gallery, each dressed for the occasion, he in dark suit and tie, she in heavy silk that draped luxuriously over her small and fragile body. They were looking out the window, and he was putting off having a first drink. They watched as guests stepped from darkness into the swirling street light below. They came at first in ones and twos, smiling, expectant, making a night of it. Then a crowd, perhaps let off by an evening train. The room filled.

The two were soon pulled apart. Colleagues of his approached, and as he was shaking their hands she made an excuse and drifted off among the other guests. He watched her go.

What a crowd, one said.

And on a night like this, said the other.

Yes, it's something, he said.

She must be pleased.

Yes, he said. I'm glad you came.

They left to see the pictures: each an identical canvas, each a singular configuration of color, building a theme, painting to painting, that seemed, if you cast your eyes quickly around the room, to embrace an entire spectrum of color.

The light in the room was warm, dim, with soft spotlights hanging from the ceiling illuminating each painting. The bright light on the wall, the repetition of rectangles, the darkness elsewhere, reminded him of a train passing in the night.

He got himself a glass of wine at the bar—real glass, a nice up-grade from the usual plastic cups at these affairs—and returned to the window.

People seemed to be enjoying the show. There was the right amount of attention to the walls, the discussion, at least on the edges, appropriately focused on matters of color and composition.

It amused him how people could come up with things to say about abstractions such as these. It wasn't that the paintings were cold. The whole show was a blur of emotion. But except for the thick paint and the textured surface, the emotion was devoid of content. Well, that wasn't true. The content was there all right. He just couldn't see how anyone else could see it. They saw what they saw, what they wanted to see, perhaps.

They did not see what he saw.

He noticed her then, across the room, standing on the edge of things, alone, watching the people look at her paintings. He tried to imagine what she was thinking, what she was feeling. He thought he knew. She was happy, he thought, but not in the facile way one would expect at a successful opening. He wasn't sure she even noticed that they had all come to see her work.

In the painter's room there was color and movement, the soft chatter of a crowd between sets at a nightclub, the darkness of bodies, the occasional brightness of a laughing face, the backdrop of pale wall and punctuated windows of color, falling, swirling.

He thought to go over, to join her there, but he didn't want to disturb her. He marveled at her ability to remain alone on such a night.

They wouldn't stay long. The gallery would understand. It was late. It was the snow. And she was tired.

WHEN SOMEONE APPROACHES *a grave-in-process, he should bring an odd number of fairly large stones in his hands, usually three, and place them on a nearby pile. The rocks will be used after the grave is filled to cover, protect, and mark it. The number is symbolic: Dasse pray and give things away in even numbers, whose evenness, or two-ness, is identified with peace and symmetry. The odd number suggests asymmetry, the absence of the deceased, the family now out of balance. Dasse speak of death as leaving a gap, a rent in the whole. Insofar as even numbers represent wholeness, odd numbers represent incompleteness.*

⁂

Her painting gave way to drawing only and finally to elemental smudges of charcoal on paper with fingers that stained the sheets of their bed and their cheeks. She could no longer manage the stairs to her basement studio. Then she could not get out of bed. On days when she had strength to sit up, she drew pictures on a table he'd rigged across the bed like a lap tray. They'd visit in the evening, lingering over supper as they had done before.

She ate in bed. She ate almost nothing.

He sat within easy reach on an old straight-backed chair.

I've been thinking, she said.

Yes.

Whether painting ever really creates a new image. More and more I think it just reassembles what's already there, however abstractly. The painter is simply a messenger.

A messenger?

Yes, a messenger, or maybe just a shell in a shell game.

Ah, you collect a bit of something, a dried pea, hide it under your nutshell for a while, then reveal it somewhere else. Like that?

Something like that. But then, not. A shell game suggests there's a master, an agent in charge. I'm not sure there's anyone quite like that. It's all so accidental.

But isn't something new expressed in the assembly and timing: when to hold, when to let go?

No, she said. I think that, too, is accidental, a matter of chance, how things come—not you, but the play of things.

Do you feel like a shell?

I don't feel in control.

Then what's the difference between what you make and the world itself, between you and what you see?

I'm sorry. What difference?

Are you tired?

Let's just lie here.

They were silent. He held her hand, felt her thumb press against his palm. Her thumb and forefinger were firm and calloused from drawing. The rest of her hand was smooth and cool and light as an empty glove.

They remained like that. Then he climbed into bed. He lay on his side beside her, pressed his forehead into hers, breathed her breath.

He wasn't convinced. But for the moment it made him feel a little better, what she said.

DIGGING GRAVES IS *difficult in all areas where I saw a burial, for the ground is littered with stones beneath as well as upon the surface. Men dig with shovels and break or loosen rocks with pickaxes. They spell each other. There are never more than two in the grave at one time. They remove sandals before they drop into the grave. They dig with bare feet. I once started down for a turn and forgot to remove my sandals. The others reminded me before I had a chance to lower myself into the hole. Men also pray in their bare feet, and during weddings, the groom makes a painful march, often for several miles, barefoot across the stones. There is another curiosity about digging graves. Men toss the earth out of the grave to the east. The wind here is incessant and strong and blows from the east, so mounding the loose soil there ensures that dirt blows back on the diggers. I suppose this is consistent with the rule about bare feet: It adds to the misery.*

VIII

Seventeen months before

He closed the book. It was Saturday, middle of the afternoon, and he had no plans for the rest of the day. The house was quiet. He could hear the fan hum, blowing a cooling breath toward her bed. A warbler somewhere chimed its raspy bell song into the afternoon heat: *sleep sleep pretty one slee-eep*. A car passed. He put the book on the stand, rose, and, so he wouldn't startle her, took the long way around the house to the bedroom, through dining room and kitchen. Months before, he'd set up their bed in the back, and then, two weeks ago, he brought in a special bed with metal rails and wheels. From here she could see the yard and the birds.

She did not turn her head as he entered. But he knew that she knew. Perhaps her body tensed. Perhaps it was the way her hands lay. He'd looked for what it was and couldn't see. Still he knew that she knew, and this pleased him. At least there was that.

How are you, sweetness?

She didn't answer.

He walked around to the foot of the bed and looked at her. Her eyes were open, blinking appropriately, but he could not say whether she saw him. He assumed she could. Her eyes were hollow and still, deep as night. They did not move.

A white sheet covered her body to her chest. Her arms, outside the sheet, lay thin and limp at her sides. She had on a clean white cotton gown that tied at the neck and opened at the back.

How about a bath?

Before, when he asked, she would smile and nod and make herself ready. They spoke then in the easy, unhurried way of old lovers.

She did not smile now.

He liked giving her baths. He thought it was the least he could do, and he thought that he owed her.

The nurse, who bathed her when he was away, used thin rubber gloves. He did not use gloves. Never had. He enjoyed the feel of the slick warm water and he enjoyed the feel of her body, and gloves would only have protected him from those feelings. Since the hospital bed came he had not slept beside her. Bathing was their last intimacy. On weekends, because he had more time, he took more time.

He thought she enjoyed the baths, too, and he thought this for the same reason he thought she knew he was in the room. He could not say how he knew, or why he assumed. It was what was left between them. He spoke the whole time, though for some days she had not spoken back. Not even a murmur. He was attentive, imagined what she would say if she spoke. He told her what he would do before he did it. He framed it as a question.

How about a bath?

He kept the toiletries under the kitchen sink because the kitchen was near the back room. He turned the hot tap on, let the water warm, and while it was running, fetched two black plastic basins from below. He also lifted several clean washcloths from a pile there and went to the bathroom near the kitchen for three or four towels that he would use to dry her and to cover clean parts of her body during the bath. He filled the basins with water, now steaming hot. He added a few drops of a mild soap to one and carried the basins and towels into the bedroom. He put these on the table beside the bed and returned to the kitchen for a bottle of scented oil, which he set in the warm water for her massage afterward.

OK if I pull the sheet down?

He untied her gown and gently pulled it out from around her. Her body was bare except for the diaper.

I'm going to lift you, all right?

She complied limply. He thought of it as cooperation.

How about if I clean you now?

He meant change the diaper. He didn't say *cleaning* for *bathing*. He didn't think she liked him cleaning her. Who would? But it had to be done. He did it easily. He'd been squeamish at first. Now cleaning her was no more troublesome than sopping up spilled milk. After cleaning came bathing, and that was different.

The diaper was empty. There have to be inputs for outputs—that's what she would have said had she spoken—and these days there were hardly any inputs. Saline solution. Pain medication. Ice shavings for her mouth.

He covered her body with the sheet, leaving just her face exposed.

She was unimaginably thin. The sheet fell across her body like canvas over tent poles. Her face alone remained beautiful as before. He had always admired her face, and though it was so different now, he thought it was even more beautiful. A face in a religious painting: pale, still, utterly unattached. This he washed with the care a priest gives the cup and bowl during Mass. With one hand he smoothed her graying auburn hair, then held the top of her head carefully to keep it steady, to reassure her, and with the other washed her forehead, her cheeks, her chin. He dabbed her eyelids, which closed, as if by magic, then reopened.

He was thorough. He knew she liked to be clean. He made sure to find the curves of her ears, to wash the oily skin at the hairline. He would not wash her hair today, as it had been washed yesterday. He dried her face, caressed her forehead, and told her he would do her legs next.

He lifted the sheet from her legs, washed each in turn. He took care to clean between her toes, the bottoms of her feet. He dried and covered her legs with a large towel and next bathed arms and torso. He cleaned her this way: face first, then legs and feet, then arms, then torso, then genitals. Then he turned her, an operation he'd learned from the nurse, and bathed shoulders and back, her arms and legs, her buttocks.

He thought about it this way: that he was painting her with water, that each stroke brought her back to life. The water restored her skin, if only for the few seconds until it dried. He touched her carefully, knowing his touch also gave her pain.

Her skin was the color of snow. He could see the blue veins beneath, like cracks in ice. Her arms and legs were thin as wintered branches. The once round breasts and hips, wrinkled and narrow.

He remembered their lovemaking, long afternoons when they would bathe and then take turns massaging each other, and with growing eagerness and hunger grab and bite and pinch and lick and taste and rub and enter careless and unexpected places, and then they seemed to devour each other, each predator, each the other's prey. These memories blew through him as breaths from the open window, raising the cotton curtains for a moment, then subsiding.

She was now, he thought, a fragile ceramic. White clay pressed thin, raku-cracked, translucent, as if someone's gaze alone would break it.

After the bath he removed the towels, pulled the sheet over her body, kissed her forehead, and told her that he would return. He took the wet towels and basins and returned with the warm oil. He hummed something softly. He could not have said what. Her eyes, still open, said nothing. He winked at them anyway. He studied her face. He remembered the fuller face—the face without sores—the thick, sensual beauty. A hungry beauty. Eyes that spoke with quick, painterly intelligence. She had been an artist. What was left was older, paler—finer than ever. This he studied as he rubbed the oil between his hands.

He bent to massage her temples with his fingertips, pressing a little against the bridge of her eyes, upper lip, and chin, caressing her throat and then the back of her neck. He kissed her forehead as he finished, pulled the sheet that had been at her neckline down to her waist, poured more warm oil into his hands, and spread it across her breasts and shoulders and strigiled the oil from her torso with his hands, careful not to squeeze. The oil, like the water before, restored her skin, if only for the moment.

This part of the bath, done for pleasure, was the most like lovemaking. It was also the least like lovemaking. So conscious was he of not hurting her that his touch was surgical. He touched every part of her body, every surface, working down from her head. He found every crevice, every bend, every hollow. He covered the regions of her body with towels as he finished. He lingered no place long, and hurried no place either. And this attention, self-conscious as it was, was concentrated and dangerous as an exotic rite. Perhaps, he thought afterward, she was more relaxed than before. Perhaps she rested better for the bath. He hoped it was true. But he could not say.

Can I get you anything? he asked when he had changed the

sheets with crisp new ones, wrapped her in a clean nightgown, covered her with the sheet, and tucked her in.

She did not answer—not, at least, in any way he could understand.

UNLESS THEY HAVE *a good excuse and elders release them, all able-bodied men in camp, as well as passersby, are expected to stop what they are doing, help to dig the grave, and remain until the job is finished. I saw a couple of young men get into trouble when they failed to notice that a grave was being dug as they passed on a journey. They were walking at least a quarter of a mile away. It was reasonable to assume that they had seen the burial in progress. Elders saw the travelers and sent a boy to fetch them. When they arrived, they were asked to explain themselves. The travelers said they hadn't seen. They said they were in a hurry on business for their father. The men argued back and forth for ten or fifteen minutes. The elders said: Are we not also your fathers? In the end, the travelers put in a few minutes' worth of work and were allowed to leave with stern words to keep their eyes open.*

IX

The present

The afternoon sky was white and thin. The sun, a nipple behind sheer haze. The breeze smelled of ocean. The fresh air, in spite of the heat, felt pleasant on his skin. His body was sticky with sweat and dust. He hadn't had a bath since Maikona. He'd cleaned his teeth and doused his face, but nothing more. So with the idea of finding water he set off alone to the *lagga* to wash some underwear and himself in one of its pools.

Elema was away, across the border, trying to buy an automatic rifle for protection against hyenas and thieves. He had no idea where Ali was, probably off with boys his own age tending camels. The rest were either working or relaxing inside tents or snoozing in the shade or off with grazing animals. The camp looked deserted, the tents a row of coconut halves in an abandoned shell game.

He set off across the stones to the *lagga*. He could not see the *lagga* from camp. He could not see the trees that grew down along its banks. He knew it must be near, for the women had walked there in the morning to get water. The journey took them only a couple of hours, and they would have lingered, visited, and bathed.

The path between the rocks was obvious, the earth black and soft. Mud clung to his sandals like mortar. In places it was so soft and deep that it sucked the sandals off his feet, so he carried them and continued barefoot. He remembered a photograph he'd seen in a magazine years ago. It was a man—he couldn't remember where—whose job it was to mix clay and straw with his feet for building houses. All day the man trudged in a vat of wet clay. He was bearded and old, and his feet, after a lifetime on soft, squishy earth, were deformed, long and twisted, the feet of a frog.

He left the camp alone. He worried that someone would follow. Then, as he got farther from camp, he wondered why no one followed. He wondered, what did they think? Did they want him to stay? Did they wish he would leave? Then it occurred to him that they would think he was wandering off to shit, so of course they did not follow. He did not want to be followed.

⁂

He remembered another walk to another *lagga* many years before with Abudo. It was a day, like this one, after a rare torrential rain. They'd gone to the *lagga* to see what the storm had brought, to see the water. Abudo wanted to show him a *lagga* after the rain.

Ab', he said. *Lagga wolin deme. Nuyas*.

He didn't really have a choice. He didn't mind. He was glad they wanted him along.

There were five or six of them. They picked their way across the rubble. There was no direct path to the *lagga* from that camp, and they had had to jump from rock to rock. The rocks were coarse, not slippery, but their wet feet slipped in the tire sandals. Their feet slid right out of the sandals. They all soon had cuts and scrapes on their toes and heels. He especially. He bled a lot, and it added to the slipperiness. The blood ran dark over the black rubber. The others were surer and faster over the rocks. He stumbled along behind as fast as he could. Now and then Abudo waited for him, and the others must have slowed their pace, for the gap never widened beyond a certain distance. Why must they go so fast? he thought, his big toe slamming sloppily into another rock. He strove to belong by being as capable as they in the desert, to be at least as good as they. And he wasn't. He never would be. They accepted him nonetheless, or tolerated him. They didn't make fun of his slowness. They were patient.

The *lagga* had steep banks, like a canyon, carved by generations of water, little by little, through the desert floor. A swale on the camp side made it easy to get down to the bottom. The ground fell gradually, like a boat ramp between docks at a lake. They walked down the scree of the slope into the *lagga*, then turned downstream, along the shore. There were trees, a forest glade. In places the trees were taller than the walls, and from a distance the *lagga* looked like a hedge meandering across the flat yellow land. The trees followed the water's path south to the Chalbi salt flats. Two thousand years before, the Chalbi had been a lake with fish in it. Now it was a desert. Except once or twice every couple of years after a heavy rain when the *lagga* flowed: Then it was a sea of mud.

There was water in the *lagga* but plenty of bank for walking. It smelled of damp clay, like a potter's studio. The debris of old trees and mud and even rocks hung high in the branches. Water must have been terribly fierce in the night. The ravine looked harmless enough now. But he knew from experience that rivers got their water from elsewhere, that current conditions mattered less than conditions upstream. Years ago he'd nearly lost her in a deluge from upstream. So he worried now about a flash flood. If there was rain in the highlands to the north, they might not know it, and water could come and trap them where banks were steep.

The *lagga* turned to the left.

When they rounded the bend they found a woman's body in the branches of a tree.

At first they'd thought it was an animal, an antelope. He was fascinated to see. Then he realized it was a woman and he started, and then, for a moment, it was his wife, and he started again, unable to breathe, and then it wasn't her at all, she was safe in Marsabit, but it was a woman. He didn't want to look. He couldn't stop himself.

For a few moments he and his companions didn't know where to look. They looked at each other and then away. They looked elsewhere, into the trees. Abudo pointed out a desert hare that had been pinned to an acacia nearby; a thorn pierced its eye. He stared at the rippling, windblown surface of the water. He wondered whether there were fish. He'd read about mud puppies, amphibious fish that slept deep in the clay until a rain, then emerged, like the phoenix, to swim in the water and mate on its slimy edges.

The body was still there.

He thought of the horror she must have felt when she was caught in the current, unable to swim. But the ability to swim would not have helped. It wouldn't have mattered if she knew how. The water would have dragged her into a tree one way or the other.

She looked wide awake. Her mouth was open as if to speak.

The others knew the woman. She was Gumato Kalacha, from a satellite camp near Tulu Bore. She was a widow. She kept sheep and goats. She had grown children. Her daughter was a beggar in Isiolo. Two sons were teachers, one of them at a government high school in the capital.

It disturbed the men in the *lagga*, the thought of handling her. They did not want to touch her and wanted to call women from camp to do it. Not because she was nearly naked, her clothes pulled from her body by the current, but because she was dead. They did not want to touch her deadness. For people who knew little of germs, let alone about washing them off a cup or a spoon, their wanting to avoid touching a body, even one that had been washed down a river, seemed to him an incipient sense of contagion, one the men preferred to inflict on women.

Adano, one of Abudo's friends, didn't see the point of going back. He suggested they handle her with cloth.

Adano sat on the anthropologist's shoulders and tried to lift the body from the branches, but the thorns held her. The thorns made it difficult to pull her out. They had to put a second man atop another's shoulders and lift and then pull. It took some coordination.

The branches held back what remained of her clothes, and she came away from the tree naked, clad only in her metal jewelry, which glinted like silver in the sun. She was not heavy, but the men above had been unable to hold the awkward weight, and he and the other man standing below had tried to catch the body. In the end it had fallen like a stillborn calf into the pooled water beneath them.

She was old, made of tent poles and flaps of dried leather. Her face was smooth, however, and here she did not look at all dead. He half expected her to wake up and complain about the way they were mishandling her.

Abudo, now resigned to the chore, lifted her out of the water and sat her on a flat stone in some shade up the bank. He straightened her out as best he could. He smoothed her hair with the palm of his hand. He did not try to close her eyes. He covered her with his cloth.

She must have been crossing the *lagga* in the storm. That meant she had been trying to get back to camp with her flock. Somewhere in the *lagga* there would be bodies of goats and sheep.

Her body was stiff. It did not smell.

Abudo sent Adano to camp to call others to help carry the body and to organize sending a message to her own camp. They waited under a tree upstream and talked of bodies they had seen and the different expressions on their faces.

They agreed that Gumato's face looked alive.

One of the men said it was normal, in death, for women to look more alive than men.

He thought there was an expert in every crowd.

Abudo said the woman was rich with goats and had always been generous, helping others by giving them goats. He said she'd been a big person, *nama gudha*, using the masculine gender.

He noted the unusual attribution and made a note to himself to write it down when they got back in camp.

The other man, who had made the observation about the liveliness of dead women, said she was not *nama gudha*, she was a woman, *niitii*.

Abudo said that was so, but now she was sleeping.

DIGGING FINISHED, THE *men return to the tent for the body, which has already been prepared and placed atop a litter made of* korbo, *a wicker-like panel between public and private spaces inside the tent. Poles for loading camels, or for bracing the rear windward wall of the tent, are used for the litter. Men hold a muslin cloth over the shrouded body as a sort of canopy. They take pains to be sure that the canopy covers the body from tent to grave and while the body is lowered into the grave. They lift and lower the litter three times at the house, presumably to demonstrate a reluctance to remove it. Again at the grave, they lift and lower the litter three times. As men lower the body, those holding the canopy remain above and keep the cloth shaking. They offer no explanation for the shaking cloth.*

X

Sixteen months before

He did not speak at the funeral. Others remarked on his silence. He was unmoved by the ritual. His work exposed him to the funerary customs of dozens of societies, all in many ways different, and he could think of no particular reason why any tradition, including his own, was better, more comforting, than another. He understood the need to dispose of the body. He supposed the rituals were meant to help people manage their feelings. He didn't want to manage his feelings. Let them be. And grief was not his only feeling. Not all of what he felt was as understandable as grief. Death is a strange betrayal. The dead leave the living more certainly than if they'd run off with a lover. You cannot blame them. Even if they were reckless or killed themselves, it's not obvious that they got, or even sought, the better deal. It's not wrong to die, not the way it's wrong to renege on a promise or deceive someone. There's no final accounting. No way to meet up later and talk about it over coffee. Who could say whether you deserved to be abandoned? Or didn't? The dead are just gone. They cannot defend themselves. You're free to think and feel whatever you want. That's the hell of it.

⁂

One week after, a woman stopped at the house. She'd been his wife's friend, not close, but a friend who sat with her in the final days, when he was teaching and couldn't be there himself. The woman was an artist. She knew his wife through a gallery that showed both of their paintings. He asked her in, invited her to sit, offered tea, which she refused.

They sat opposite, avoiding each other's eyes. The woman wept. Her tears embarrassed them both. He handed her a box of tissues. He did not cry. Not then. And she did not understand his silence. He was no help. When she rose he rose, too, wanting only that she leave.

You were brave, she said at last.

He wasn't sure how to respond.

She was the brave one, he said.

But you stayed. Well, you know, some wouldn't. It can't have been easy.

I don't know what you mean.

How she died.

Yes.

You were there for her.

I owed her that much.

No one owes anyone that much.

It's not like you count these things up, is it?

I suppose not. It was good. You were good.

Good was the last thing I was.

She did not answer.

They were still standing.

I should go.

Yes. OK.

Take care.

Yes. You, too.

He watched from the window as she walked to the car, got in, and pulled away. It wasn't fair. She would not know why he was being difficult and would wonder what she might have said or done. He should have said something.

⁂

In the following weeks, colleagues stopped to speak in the hall, their concern worn like a costume. It wasn't that they were insincere. They just didn't feel the loss. She'd been a private woman, an infrequent face at dinner parties. The manner of her death didn't help. They wondered about his health but didn't ask. He'd have had an answer. Her doctors said that some people simply possessed a natural immunity. They didn't understand how or why. He'd been lucky. Or unlucky. It depended how you looked at it. Friends volunteered to visit or suggested he come to dinner. But they didn't, and he didn't. He said he was fine. What was he supposed to say? He was alive. Eventually the inquiries came to an end. He returned to his office where the door remained open and he alone. It was awkwardness at first, then habit. He was elsewhere. You couldn't blame him. He went through the motions, met classes, advised students, attended faculty meetings, returned home at the end of the day. He was civil. He just wasn't there anymore.

IN THE CASE *of a man, his firstborn son—or, ideally, the firstborn of his firstborn—holds the head as the body is lowered into the grave and placed in the lower chamber. In the case of a woman, her husband holds the head. This person also places tobacco and salt near the head and puts a rock under it as a pillow. Both men and women are laid in the grave with heads pointing north. A woman is placed on her left side, facing east, while a man is placed on his right side, facing west. Left is the feminine side of the body; right is the masculine side. Dasse say that these positions reflect positions men and women assume in sex: on their right and left sides. Even in death, Dasse are preoccupied with fertility.*

XI

Nine months before

He could not bear at first to see or touch anything of hers—then he could not bear not to. Death would not be sad if desire died, too. He sat in her studio and stared at the unfinished paintings on the wall, which had hung there since the illness made it impossible for her to work. He opened the drawers of her chest in the bedroom and arranged her socks, her underwear, her sweaters. He spent an entire day and most of the night looking at old photographs, not eating or drinking or answering the phone. Even in the late stages of illness when she was no more than a wintry stalk of herself she had smelled the same. He did not wash her pillowcase until he'd spent so much time resting his head on it that it no longer smelled of her. He worried that he would forget her smell, her voice, her face, her touch. She died over and over that way—in fragments and gestures, eroding day by day like the bank of a river.

⁂

She'd kept a journal. Not of words but images: lines, drawings, smudges, splashes of color. These were her stock in trade, a record of days, thoughts, impressions, appreciations. The journal was to her what the field notes he kept were to him: a place to record observations, work up thoughts, occupy hands and eyes in a public place. If she was having coffee downtown, she might see a cheek she liked, the way the down of pale hair faded toward the ear, or the way the curve rose and broke and fell to the chin like half a heart. Perhaps it was a child, sipping chocolate, or a dark stranger with iced espresso. She'd pull the journal from her satchel, sketch the face, the hand, the torso, and go back to her coffee.

She noticed small things. Sometimes, it was just a line. A line with a slight curve to it. A line with a quiver. A line with an arc, a twist, a loop. A line as straight as a ruler, beside a line as straight as a stalk of wheat, or a line as bent as a vine. They were lines among an infinite number of lines in front of her, lines she'd identified, pulled out, redefined, documented and recorded.

It was, in a way, a kind of analysis. In the reality before her eyes, this was what she noticed, separated out, found interesting. It wasn't always clear what she had documented: whether it was something out there in the world or an inspiration she'd had over a creamy latte.

She'd sketch objects: wine bottles, napkins, bottle caps, crackers. She drew people, usually without their knowing. That way they were less self-conscious, less stiff. Her gaze was a powerful thing. It inhibited him the few times she drew his face. He didn't like it when she did, but then he didn't like it when she didn't.

She traveled with a small watercolor kit—a tin box containing cups of color and a couple of brushes—and a quart-sized plastic bottle with water to wet the brushes, or she'd use the water in a water glass at the restaurant. She would wash sketches with color, realistically or wildly. There was no way of predicting. Once, early in their marriage, she showed him a sketch in which she'd rendered him, despite his European ancestry, as an African. She mixed things up like that. She painted auburn clouds and purple leaves and golden waters. It was as if, in creating these fictions, she altered reality, made it more accessible to others. They'd talked about this and disagreed. For her it was all the same. The truth, she'd said, was in the telling. The paper was its own reality. He could not say where the fiction came from, but he could not let go of the difference between fiction and nonfiction. Whatever she drew was from out there or in here or some combination. He disliked the idea of it not mattering. It didn't matter to him that she was true to the world she painted. It wasn't objectivity he clung to. It was the slipperiness of no difference: her unwillingness to say that the drawing came either from her own head or from the world she observed. She didn't like to make the distinction.

ONCE THE BODY *is in the recess at the bottom of the grave, men lower stone slabs into place, forming an inclined roof of sorts over the body. Others on the surface mix water with dirt and hand the mud to those below, who use it as mortar to seal cracks between the slabs. This done, the grandson, or son, or husband, climbs to the surface and flicks a bit of earth from the mound into the grave, using the pinky finger of his left hand—the least finger of the lesser hand. Then the men take turns shoveling dirt into the grave, much as they had taken turns digging it. On top they fashion a substantial mound of stones. The burial finished, the men wash the dirt of the grave from themselves, a pragmatic as well as ritual cleansing and a significant sacrifice of precious water.*

XII

Three months later he could no longer smell her on the pillow. He sat one afternoon, the usual time, on the bottom stair to her studio. Just sitting. He enjoyed the light, with the overheads off, the angled late afternoon sun through the southern windows.

Her journals were arranged like encyclopedias, tall and uniform, so different inside, on a shelf beneath a paint-stained green table in a corner, under a wall of books. The journals were private. She'd been clear about that from the start. Early in their marriage when they were young, not long out of college, he'd wondered what she was drawing and looked. The current journal had been on her desk in the back room off the kitchen. He'd asked about the last drawing, said he liked it.

You looked?

What?

I can't believe you did that.

He was startled. She wasn't angry so much as surprised herself. Perhaps that had the greater effect on him than if she'd been angry. He had done something shameful, like a child, without knowing.

I didn't know it mattered.

Of course it matters. What would you think if I rummaged in your journal?

I wasn't rummaging. I just looked. I was admiring. They're drawings. They're beautiful drawings. You want people to see your paintings—why wouldn't you want me to see your drawings?

You say that like drawings are the same as paintings.

Well?

The drawings are private.

Really? They're sketches.

Of course. That's what makes them private. My paintings are rehearsed. They're worked over. They're abstractions. They're theoretical, in a way. Surely you get that. But drawings come fresh out. Right then, there. Spontaneous, immediate. Don't you see?

They were young and naïve about conversations like this. But that was not the reason it escalated. They had not yet learned to fight. Their feelings were beneath the surface. She found it easier than he to keep track of them, to know what they were. His feelings tended to startle him.

The thing was, looking back, he realized even then that it was wrong to look in her journal. He just didn't think she'd mind *him* doing it. They were married. No secrets. He wouldn't have wanted her looking in his own journal, if for no other reason than his writing there was unrehearsed. But he didn't think it would have bothered him as much as it did her. He didn't think his journal writing was true, or truer than writing he'd had a chance to correct.

That was a difference between them. His writing wasn't real until finished, smoothed out. For her, the drawings were more real incomplete, accidental, and spontaneous. They came from different geographies on this; the logic of the one violated that of the other. He was not to look. Her drawings were private, unless she chose to show them.

They hardly seem worth protecting, he'd said.

That's the point, she'd shot back.

He didn't see.

THE CHALBI DESERT *is strewn nearly everywhere with volcanic rubble. Rocks are common as air. There is ancient precedence in the region for stone burial mounds. There are hundreds of sizable cairns, some fifteen feet tall and thirty or more feet in diameter, a few, at least, dating back nearly four thousand years. Excavations of the graves show that, for all this time, men and women here have been buried on their sides, heads pointing north, faces east or west. The ancient cairns, as well as the more modest contemporary ones, are larger than necessary to protect graves from scavengers, such as hyenas and jackals, which would dig up a body if they could. One can only speculate about the motives of their makers to mark, preserve, remember.*

◆

So it was with trepidation that he looked. He touched the books tentatively, as if she might return, catch him. When he remembered this moment months later, as he gazed out over the desiccated plains where sadness ran on endlessly, he realized she must have wanted him to see. She intended him to know these things.

But the first time, he was ashamed.

He pulled a volume off the shelf. It dated back to before they knew each other. Then another and another. He saw what the journals revealed. It wasn't any particular drawing so much as the pattern, the subject matter, the themes that came and went. She drew dogs, and then people as dogs, and then dogs as people, and then birds. The lines of faces became abstract and then it was all line and color, like doodling, and now and then he recognized the foundation of a painting that he'd liked. There were probably plenty of paintings to recognize in the journals, but he lacked the eye or sufficient memory. Why hadn't he paid closer attention?

There were times when she'd worked in colors: setting one against another, against another, like color cards at the paint store. There were times when she seemed to break in a pencil, watching the point dull, so she'd know the life of a sharpened pencil, know how fast the brittle point rounded and thickened and provided the line she wanted, and for how long. Or in a similar way learned how much pressure to apply for what sort of line. She was like a singer practicing a note, an athlete rehearsing a movement again and again, until there was no effort at all in recreating it perfectly. Between these worksheets she'd sometimes drawn faces of people they knew.

In the eighth or ninth volume he found his face. It had been sketched, he thought, at a party they'd attended, before they'd become a couple. He was playing a guitar. He didn't know she'd drawn that, couldn't say whether she did it from memory or drew it on the spot. Later, there were drawings of him without clothes, of him without clothes with her, of him making love to himself, to her, to a friend of theirs. Then there were only genitals, then lines, curves, shadows.

The weather changed. She stopped drawing him. There were few pictures of him after those early days when they'd discovered themselves as a couple, established a reality together, got used to the idea, the habit, of each other. Then there were no more. He was hurt and embarrassed. He was her husband, her partner, and regardless of what had happened, they had each been the center of the other's life. How could she not have drawn pictures of him? He could not stop thinking about himself. What did it matter? Here was a document, evidence of her interests. Did the fact she stopped drawing him mean he did not matter? Does matter need evidence? He'd written about her in his own journal. They'd been together more than twenty years, and only in the first two—most of that time before they were married—did she draw him. Her drawings were fantasies. Had he not been part of her fantasy life? What was he in the end—nurse, friendly ear, someone who demanded too much or too little from her, even when she was dying?

And why had she died?

He skipped a number of volumes, years ahead, and opened the first of a half dozen or so that spanned their longest period of fieldwork together.

The one, he thought, that had sentenced her.

The drawings were now a study of contrasts: pastel landscapes on one page and jagged dark charcoal details of thorn scrub on the next. Nearly all the bushes and trees had thorns. There was a bush called the wait-a-bit bush because of its clutching cat-like claws. There were bushes with straight thorns and long thorns and thorns like tiny saw teeth. She drew faces of people, shrouded at first behind veils, then, as she got to know them, uncovered, full faces. There were pictures of Dasse friends, Ado and Abudo and their children, drawn in artists' crayons, almost like oils. She'd never turned these into paintings. Ado and Abudo would not have appreciated paintings. Their house was a tent and lacked walls for such things. They lacked the necessary training to see drawings, paintings, even photographs as representations.

He turned the page. On one side was a drawing of their home at the mission: a cinder-block structure with an iron-sheet roof and metal window frames. An open veranda, running the length of the building, connected the rooms. There was an outhouse bath and toilet. The mission had a pump, and well water was lifted to a reservoir in a tall block structure and from there gravity-fed to five of the six buildings in the complex: the priest's house, still occupied by the old priest; the nun's house, vacant; the kitchen, where a local woman came daily to cook for the priest; the clinic, staffed two mornings a week by a woman who had done a six-month course in practical nursing, as well as one day a year by a flying doctor. The doctor was an eighty-year-old Swiss woman who swore like a bandit and, to the great alarm of her passengers, napped on long flights while she flew. And their house. The house was a row of tiny rooms. They lived in two small rooms at one end, using one for kitchen and the other for bedroom. Off the porch was another, larger room, which he used as a study, where he wrote and stored equipment and things he collected. It was also a storeroom for the mission. The next room over she used as a studio. Its single merit was that it had a door she could close and behind which be alone.

She had drawn the building in pencil and then washed it with watercolor. It was quite accurate. It must have been during a rainy season—a time he spent longer periods in the camps, away from her. It was easier to travel then, for water could be found in riverbeds and there was plenty of milk for guests. The sky behind the house had the low clay-colored clouds of the rainy season. She caught the mood perfectly. He could almost smell the clammy dust in the air, like a tidal marsh, like the seashore—an unusual odor in the desert, where the air tended to be dry and clear and lifeless as sand.

On the next page was a portrait of Abudo, his friend and informant.

He was not jealous by nature, but jealousy is a feeling of want, and at the moment he was empty. He wanted her, wanted her more than he had wanted her when she was alive. Of course he did: wanting is never as acute as wanting what one does not have. She was dead. He had lost himself.

Now this.

Here was his wife, his partner, his best friend, drawing pictures of herself with another man.

Here was his friend—yes, Abudo had been a friend, though he winced in the moment to think it. They'd walked together across the desert for days on end and sipped tea before a fire under a solitary tree surrounded by a globe of vibrating stars. A world divided them—language, history, economy—yet they'd enjoyed each other's company, stood together when others might have flagged.

Ali al. Out is out. That's what Abudo had said.

Yes, they'd been friends.

And here was Abudo, in various states of arousal, alone and with her, kneeling at her back in one, lying thin and sinewy between her legs in another, dark coppery flanks against paper-white thighs.

Could they have imagined this?

Could she have done this?

His life, his love, had drawn such pictures, thought such thoughts. What did it mean?

She must have wanted Abudo. She must have imagined that she had wanted him, for the expression on her face in the drawings, the open mouth, the half-closed eyes, the rigor in her back, the flex of her calves and reach of her toes spoke of joy and pleasure and something they had called love.

What did it mean for him to think that she had done this, and enjoyed it? And believe all of it to be true?

There were several pages of sketches, drawings, watercolors, crayons, each of them beautiful, arousing. He felt a curious mix of emotions that ranged from shame and hurt to anger, but also excitement. His heart was racing. His penis, he discovered, was stiff. The paper was slightly textured, and he looked at the pictures first as wholes but then as parts and lines and colors and saw where she'd pressed hard, perhaps in her own excitement, and where she'd feathered the paper with a slow gentle touch. She had made love to the memory, he thought, and he found himself unfastening his own pants and touching himself and making love to that memory, their own lovemaking now shaded by that between her and Abudo, when he was, God knows, elsewhere. He lay the book down and finished, and with his climax, his face melted and he began to weep as he had not before, and at that point he could not tell whether he wept for her, for his longing for her, for her absence, or whether he cried because of this new and alienating idea of her, and of himself.

The drawings were not dated—she never dated pages in the journal, only the volume itself. This one spanned months in the field when she had suffered most. He supposed if there was a moment to be unfaithful, it was then.

THE FAMILY NEXT *places domestic objects atop the pile of grave stones: the dead person's bed; matting from the tent; a milk container, broken in two and made useless; and, if it was a man, his spear shaft, or if a woman, several poles from her tent. The man's spear shaft and the woman's tent poles are made of the same kind of wood. They are also about the same thickness, though a tent pole is more than twice as long as a spear shaft. The spear shaft is straight and associated with the penis. The shaft is a euphemism for the penis. The tent pole is curved, a shape associated with women and female products. These objects will remain atop the grave, unless blown away by the wind, until the site is swept eight or sixteen years later.*

XIII

Three and a half months before

The letter about Abudo arrived a little more than a year after her death. A pale blue aérogramme with familiar stamps from far away. The handwriting was small and spare and trembled like the high heat of the desert where it originated. The letter was written by the aging priest they'd known years before when he was doing research for his book and she was waiting, wanting at least to be in the same hemisphere as he, resenting the interruption of her own work. The priest had been a kind consolation. The priest did not know she was dead. The letter was addressed to them both.

The letter said that their friend Abudo Guyo had died. The priest wondered if they knew. He offered comforting words, said Abudo's family was doing as well as could be expected, that they'd asked about him and his wife, which had prompted him to write, on the chance that they hadn't heard. He said the drought continued and urged them to pray that rains would come. He hoped they were well. The priest would not have imagined the effect of the news.

⁂

He'd met Abudo at the Maikona wells, where he'd gone to watch the activity, meet people, make contact. Abudo was watering the family's camels, had come down off the plains the night before.

During the dry season, which is all but a few weeks out of the year, nomads must drive livestock to wells to drink. According to an elaborate schedule, each camp waters its goats and sheep every five days and camels every twelve. Since wells serve a wide area, dozens of different camps visit daily with thousands of animals. And since there are only about thirty wells at Maikona, scattered like craters across a dusty expanse the size of a few football fields, the herds are held back and watered in turns. As each group is released, the bone-thirsty animals run madly to drink what they've been able to smell, but not taste, for hours.

Nomads move around. They're hard to track down. If you want to meet one it's best to find out when his or her camp is watering stock. So in addition to the herds and their keepers at the wells, there were visitors: livestock buyers, friends, family, people arranging marriages, others collecting debts, fathers catching up with sons, mothers with daughters, idlers from the settlement nearby to watch the action. All that activity kicked up a storm of dust, and what with the wind, the area was soon shrouded in a gritty yellowish fog.

He was standing and watching beside one of the wells when a man who'd been drawing water with a plastic bucket, the bottom of an old jerry can, climbed out of the well and handed him the bucket with a big smile on his face. They'd read each other's minds. Lifting water out of a well, pouring it into a trough, bending, splashing, getting wet, and being useful were exactly what he wanted. It was 110 degrees. Getting wet was the best part.

So he joined the bucket brigade. There were three inside the well. The man he replaced stood outside where he could watch. He mimed what the newcomer was supposed to do, which the newcomer sort of knew already from watching. What he showed that the other didn't know was how to pace his effort to keep up with the animals and the others in the well without exhausting himself. A full bucket would rise to his feet from the man on the ledge below. As he handed down an empty, he'd grab the full one and lift it over his head and pour it into the trough. Over and over.

After about an hour the camels were finished drinking, and it was time to move aside so another camp could water its herds.

They rested in the shade of a nearby thorn tree and drank water laced with milk, which was surprisingly refreshing. It was only about a month into his fieldwork. His language was lousy. But it turned out that the man who'd smiled spoke the national language, and for another hour or so they asked and answered each other's questions. The other's name was Abudo. His companions put up with the intrusion in part, he thought, because he'd helped, which generated good feelings.

A door opened. Abudo told him when he would return with the herds. He promised in turn to help. The meeting was accidental. It couldn't have been scripted more perfectly to initiate a field relationship.

The next time Abudo came he brought his new friend an *ororo*, a man's staff, made of the chestnut-colored wood of a fruit-bearing tree. All adult men carried an *ororo*—much the way executives in cities back home wore ties. It was part of the uniform. Dasse men received one at their wedding. Men were constantly wondering why he didn't carry some sort of stick. He was married, wasn't he? When the two had talked under the thorn tree that first time, he'd asked Abudo where he could find an appropriate tree and cut such a staff for himself. He didn't care what kind of wood it was. He wanted a stick. He wanted to fit. Abudo said he'd cut one and bring it. He figured Abudo would lop a branch off a tree and hand it over. No big deal. Then he would peel the bark himself, carve away its bumps, sand it, rub it with oil. He looked forward to the task.

Instead, Abudo brought him a finished *ororo*. Just like that.

Over the coming weeks the two got to know each other this way, and the foreign anthropologist began visiting Abudo in his camp, which was then only about an hour's walk from Maikona. Abudo killed a goat for him. From its right foreleg, he cut *medicha*, a strip of skin, including the dew claw, that a host gives a visitor to wear on his wrist to show he has been welcomed.

One day soon after, he was at the Maikona wells, watching and drawing water for camels. Abudo wasn't there that day. Another man asked who had given him *medicha*.

My friend, he said, naming Abudo.

Abudo's your friend? The other seemed surprised. The group of them smiled.

Ay, he said. But he wondered what they found so amusing.

What have you given him?

At the time the question seemed crass. It implied that friendship was measured by material exchange. It troubled him the rest of the day, and as he mulled it over he realized that, though Abudo had given him many things—*ororo*, *medicha*, and *sek*, an embroidered pouch for chewing tobacco and a leather thong to cinch it—he'd given Abudo nothing. Of course, he'd helped draw water for camels. But he'd never handed Abudo an object, something he could keep and show others as a sign of friendship.

The next time he saw Abudo, he gave him his pocketknife.

The friendship lasted throughout the time he and his wife were in the desert. They'd spent hours and hours talking. Abudo was a few years older. He had a great interest in and knew a great deal about Dasse culture. And, odd among his peers, he was literate, had aspired once to being a teacher. That gave them something in common. Like other classic informants in anthropology, Abudo was by experience and personality an insider who was also an outsider. And he was patient. He helped his friend to no end with information, interpretation, and companionship.

In the beginning, Abudo taught him the names of things. He remembered relaxing in the back of Abudo's wife's tent. He pointed out objects hanging on the walls inside and said their names. The visitor repeated and Abudo corrected. Later Abudo took him to *fora*, the satellite camp for the camels, and they walked for miles across the desiccated plains, just the two of them, and drank milk and blood from the camels and sang with the others in camp late into the night, and he taught him the men's songs. These trips to *fora* would become a regular practice.

Once, when his family was moving camp, Abudo asked his friend to carry his spear over to a particular woman. This was early in their relationship, and he did not yet know that she was Abudo's wife's mother. The woman accepted the spear. She thought the *ferenji* was flirting with her, so she flirted back. She admired how long and straight the spear was. And then, when she asked, he told her it was Abudo's, and she gasped and let go of it as if she'd grabbed a scorpion. A mother-in-law should not have such direct contact with her daughter's husband.

He'd looked across at Abudo and Abudo laughed.

He remembered a journey he and Abudo had taken, on foot, across the desert. They'd stopped to fix tea in the shade of a solitary tree. They rested, sipped from tin mugs, and looked out across the unbroken, windblown distance.

After a silence, Abudo said, *Ali al*. Out is out.

The words puzzled him.

He thought at first they expressed sadness. But no. Looking at his friend's face he could see it was pleasure. *Out* was less a geographical than a metaphysical place. In the end he decided Abudo's words spoke to the joy of being away, just the two of them, and all that space.

⁂

Abudo's death untethered him. If he was adrift before, he was now without sight of land. What most disturbed him, what filled his head with whirling, deafening voices and drained his heart of ballast, was to learn that Abudo had died of the same scourge that killed his wife. That fact set in motion a confusion of feeling he wasn't able to shrug off.

With the letter she died all over. He cancelled classes, holed up in the curtained house, the house they'd shared those years together, and remained in bed most of a day. For the rest of the week, he didn't bring in mail, didn't eat, slept poorly. He watched at the windows, stared at the ceiling, pulled books from shelves, thumbed their pages, and left them on tables and floors, wherever he'd been sitting. He retrieved old notes and field journals from a box in the basement and read over interviews he'd made with Abudo and sketches he'd written of daily life in camp. These led to parts of the journals where he'd written of her and the difficulties she'd had living with him there. All of it made him think of the pointlessness, the sacrifice of time and energy, the damage.

At the end of his seclusion, as he cleaned himself up, he could not bring himself to look in the mirror. He shaved by feel and, not seeing, cut himself, felt the sting of the razor on his jaw, saw the blood on his fingers. Turning then to the mirror to apply tissue to the wound, he caught sight of his eyes and for a long time could not let go of them.

He returned to campus the following week but was more elsewhere than ever, though elsewhere now had location. The idea had come to him. He would go back, as soon as the semester was over, to visit Abudo's family, to travel among people called Dasse whom he and his wife had known together, about whose rituals of life and death he had written two books and numerous articles, but mainly to see the place again where they had discovered and lost each other.

MEN NEXT FETCH *a young female goat to slaughter. This is the* ilme sod'u, *a sacrifice for the altar at the head of the grave. A special man holds the animal while the eldest son cuts its throat. After it is cooked, the men lay the meat on a section of matting, or* dasse, *from the tent, the section to be put on the grave, and carry this to the grave along with the uncooked* morra, *the white fatty peritoneum of the goat's stomach. The men eat the meat together and place the pieces of glutinous white fat on the* sod'u. *Dasse associate* morra *with childbirth as well as death. The whiteness of the* morra, *symbolically opposed to the redness of blood and meat, links it with milk and bones, the marrow of which is thought to be the source of sperm. Everyone leaves the grave after the* sod'u *ceremony, save perhaps a couple of boys to keep crows from eating the fat.*

XIV

The present

Now he was picking his way alone along a narrow trail that led from Elema's camp through rifts of hard black lava and onward across stony ground toward a deceptively flat horizon. The land perplexed him. In one sense it was wilderness, a place of wild animals, hyenas and leopards and oryx and zebra. It had looked pretty much the way it did now since before there were human beings. Even now it was easy to imagine the place without people. There were few enough of them. You could walk for days and see no one. Yet the paths—arteries pressed between the clotted lava—were ancient. The region had been inhabited by humans longer than any other on earth. And what humans lived here must always have stepped along these paths. He could not begin to explain the thrill the thought gave him. It did not thrill the current residents. He amused them when he spoke about it. They listened and smiled. How could anyone know such things?

No one remembered a time before the paths. Dasse attributed them to a mythic race of giants called Wardaa, rumored to have dwelt in the area long ago. For no known reason, though one could guess it had something to do with an encroaching desert, the ancients left hundreds of years before and moved south and east toward the ocean. They were thought to be ancestors of the current population there, who spoke a language still intelligible to the people here.

The sun was hot. He'd picked the time carefully for his walk, when most of the others in Elema's camp were resting and waiting out the worst of the breathless afternoon, which made even the crows retreat into the bushes. He didn't especially like heat, but he found, much to his relief, that he could bear it. He was getting used to it again. There would be tree shade in the *lagga* and, he hoped, water to lie in. He looked back and could no longer see the tents.

The walls of the *lagga* were steep and shaley. He skirted them and found a slope he could manage. No one had warned him, but he knew to be wary of snakes that might have been swept down by the water. A cobra lived in Elema's camp. He had not seen it. Elema told him. One of the families there belonged to a lineage forbidden to harm snakes—in fact, they set out bowls of milk for the cobra to drink. Word was the snake would not harm members of this and other designated lineages. Despite its deadly venom, the snake symbolized life. It shed its skin, was reborn each year; it was immortal. He did not belong to a special lineage, did not feed the snake, enjoyed no immunity. Snakes were about the only thing he worried about. A bite from one would almost certainly end his life.

He walked carefully along the riverbed. The water no longer flowed, but there was standing water, ponds here and there along the ravine. Below a drop, where rushing water had gouged out a pool, the water was deep. He came upon a large pool. He eased his way down off a ledge beside it.

The water was the color of milky tea. There was scum on top. He left his clothes on a stone and slipped into the water. He did not dive. He did not know how deep the water was. He could not see whether the river had pushed rubble or branches into the pool. He dogpaddled slowly and carefully into the middle, keeping his head above water. The water was deep. Emboldened, he closed his eyes and sank beneath the surface. He hung there for a moment and wished he could hold his breath longer, could remain in the cool darkness. He was seldom alone. He suffered for it. It was the hardest part of camp life.

He paddled across the water, pushing scum to the side, clearing a path in front, careful not to swallow.

He thought how strange it was that he had become an anthropologist. He liked people. But he liked them in small doses. Allowed to obey his own inclinations, he might have retreated more frequently to write up what he learned and returned later for follow-up observations and interaction. In the early days of the discipline—and he could think of plenty of cases since—anthropologists had worked like biologists. They studied behaviors. They studied people the way others studied elephants or monkeys: They carried clipboards and notepads and cameras and observed and counted and saw what their subjects ate and how they prepared it. Data. There was no pretense of living with the people they studied. They returned to their tents at the end of the day, poured themselves a drink, propped their feet up, and read a book. That was no longer how it was done. Long ago, anthropologists decided to get off their colonial verandas and live with the people they studied. It was an obvious idea. One could even imagine joining up with them, not going back. It was entirely possible. It seemed as if every other day, even when his wife was with him, some crone suggested he marry her daughter. They might have been joking. But the humor hung on a possibility. Everything in his experience told him that only by living with people, being with them at all hours and over days and months, could he even begin to understand.

The problem was holding onto himself with all that company.

❖

He turned on his back. He smiled at the coolness of his body in the water. He savored being naked and alone. And as he became aware of being alone he lost the pleasure of it. He looked up at the rocks to confirm, to check. Was he alone? Had anyone followed?

The hyena stood on the ledge fifteen feet away.

Startled, he pulled himself up straight in the water with a sweep of his hands. He was not frightened, not entirely. He was a little scared. He was fascinated. He did not think the hyena would attack in daylight. He'd never heard of such a thing. What was a nocturnal animal doing out in the heat of day? He'd seen them in daylight but always at dawn, never midday.

The hyena didn't pant. It didn't sit. It stood. It didn't seem to look at him but in his general direction, regarding not him but the whole scene. It lifted its head once or twice, testing for odors. It made no sound. Then it turned and climbed the rise behind and disappeared.

The hyena must have been traveling, he thought, and come upon him in the *lagga*, maybe even thought about getting a drink, and been as surprised by him as he was by it. He was thrilled to have seen the hyena. A wild animal. Nature. He would tell them back in camp that he'd seen the hyena. He would not share his excitement. They wouldn't understand. A hyena was dangerous and evil, an animal to be killed, not wondered at. The anomaly of the hyena stirred his imagination, sent ripples across its surface, where, like the pond of muddy water, there were no obstacles except the shore itself.

I paddle in the water, look up, and Ado stands where the hyena had been. She speaks. She wants help. She tells me how poor she is. She sits on a rock. She draws with a stick in the soil. She does not look at me. She whines about her sadnesses. It is her voice that says it, not her words. Now and then she looks at me sideways with a willing and knowing smile. The smile is grotesque, and produces an effect opposite what she must have intended, linking sexual interest with her complaints, her needs. I am not aroused as I might have been but offended, saddened. I tell her I can give her money, enough for a few sheep or goats, that I will speak with NGOs in Marsabit about getting her a grant or some aid for animals.

She goes back.

My imagination is not finished. She does not go back. We have sex beside the pool. In the pool. It is sad, perfunctory, shameful, furtive as the hyena's glance, interrupted by children who have come with kids and goats to water. She pulls away, adjusts her skirt, slips off into the bush and back to camp. I will see her there and she will look at me when she brings me tea.

I do not go back to the camp right away but wait in the water. I sink into its chocolaty brownness. The bottom is slippery with clay, and I hang there, letting my breath out, seeing nothing.

Then again, it might have been otherwise. We do not make love. Instead, while I paddle around the pool, naked, afraid to come out with her on the shore, she steps down to the edge and removes the shoulder strap to her dress and squats beside the water and bathes herself. It is the most beautifully choreographed dance I have ever seen, elegant, efficient, not a needless motion, not a drop of water out of place.

I watch her. She does not look at me. She bathes. I swim. I watch but do not stare.

She finishes, stands, ties the strap of her dress at her left shoulder, picks up the clothes that she must have washed in another pool, and walks back to camp.

⁂

Imagination takes many directions, often wrong. Sometimes it gets things right. He looked up from his reverie to see a human figure descending from the edge of the plain. It was a woman, but he did not know who. She was coming from the direction of Abudo's camp. She carried a bundle under one arm, probably clothes to wash. She walked slowly, erect and mindful, picking her way among the rocks and slippery scree. It was neither the hunched trod of an old woman, resigned and deliberate, nor the careless step of a youth. The wind caught the widow's scarf she wore around her head and across her face and waved the loose end behind her like a flag.

To get to the riverbed, she turned and followed a path that took her farther north behind a rise and an outcropping of rock. He thought that, whoever she was, she had seen him and she would go to another pool. He did not get out of the water and dress. He dived instead and turned and twisted like an otter, the way they play in still waters. He surfaced with a gasp, eyes closed, drawing both hands across forehead and crown to slick back his hair. He opened his eyes and saw Ado standing beside the pool.

She looked at him and looked through him, surely aware of him but not intent on him. He was startled and said nothing. Not *ijole urgoftu.* Not fancy meeting you here. He felt he'd been caught in an illicit act but could not think what. Perhaps being alone.

She stopped looking at him and set her laundry on the ground. It was tied in a single cloth.

She stepped to the water's edge, onto a stone shelf that extended into the water. She removed her sandals, one at a time, first the right and then the left, placing them beside her feet. She knelt, her covered knees pointing to the side, her left arm holding the bank, and dipped her right arm into the water and lifted it full to her forehead and drew her wet hand down over her dry face.

The water shined on her skin like silver. Droplets fell back into the pool. She repeated this gesture, washing her face and neck. She washed, and then with the curve of her thumb and hand she pressed the water from her face. She unhitched the harness of her dress, which was tied over her left shoulder, and the cloth fell to her lap and exposed her breasts, which were round and smooth, the size of pears. It was not a sexual gesture. Breasts were not the same here as they were at home. No more erotic than a pair of knees. They were beautiful nonetheless. She washed her shoulders and arms with her right hand and then, with that arm on the bank to steady her, with her left hand. She filled her hand with water, making a ladle of her fingers, and poured it over the skin of her other arm, so the water ran down her arm. She poured water in this way over her shoulders and over her breasts. Then with her free hand she pressed the water away. She ladled water from the pool and poured it over her feet, which were smooth and hard as polished stone. She wetted the lower parts of her shins and strigiled the water to her feet. She rubbed her heels and toes, freeing the dust from within the scallops and crevices.

She did not pause when she finished. She retied the dress at her shoulder, still kneeling. She stood, slipped into her sandals, turned, picked up her bundle of clothes, and walked away, erect, indifferent, heading north along the still water, her feet making a scratching sound in the pebbles and sand. She might not have seen him. How could she not have seen him?

He lingered where he was, treading the surface, watching her go. Then he let himself sink into the muddy water. He let out the air of his lungs so his body would sink, held what little remained, and hung suspended, just above the bottom. The bottom, he knew, was slippery with clay. There he drifted as long as he could, holding his breath, seeing nothing.

EARLY THAT NIGHT, *an hour or so after sunset, the dead man's wife comes alone to the grave. This is her first visit. By now her head is completely shaved, the first time it has been cut since her wedding night. She wears a white cloth as a shawl over her head, a sign of mourning. With coals she brings from her tent, she kindles a small fire at the head of the grave, beside the* sod'u *altar. The fire links death, marriage, and childbirth, for they are the only occasions when fires at the main camp are lit outdoors. Then she returns alone to the tents.*

XV

Weeks before

So what'll it be?

The woman wore reading glasses and an oversized white shirt, like a painter's smock, rolled at the sleeves. She stood beside the table. He hadn't seen her coming.

Bacon and eggs? Sausage?

No, thanks. Just some oatmeal. And more coffee. Please.

He sat in a booth with red vinyl cushions and a white Formica tabletop with ink stains on the surface and coagulated ketchup in the cracks. It was the morning before his flight. He was thinking of the day, just a month before, when he got the letter from the priest about Abudo. That morning, before he found the aérogramme in his mailbox, he'd felt almost normal again. His grief for her had spilled its banks, spread out, and seeped in. He'd slogged through. Time healed.

He adjusted. But the letter brought everything back. Doubled it. The day began one way and ended another: A baton was passed in a race, and he was no longer the one but the other, and the other knew he wasn't going to win, wasn't even sure he could finish.

He sipped his coffee and remembered how the day one month ago had begun, the day in class, before he found the letter.

The glass door opened to the outside and let in the early morning cold. Students entered by ones and twos, tentative, half asleep, dropping to chairs with grumpy carelessness. A few smiled. One, a former blonde with ink-black hair, nose ring, black denim, skin the color of thin milk, sat in the back where she usually sat. She probably hadn't slept. But she was awake. She'd had her coffee. She didn't smile. Her left leg, hung over the right, bounced to the rhythm of a dripping faucet. She spoke more than the others and probably read more, so it was good she sat behind—her voice back there brought the rest of them into the circle whether they participated or not.

They'd been talking about a book, published nearly a century before, by a Pole who became a Brit, then went to live out World War I on islands off the coast of New Guinea. The book was a prolegomenon of modern fieldwork. Old-fashioned as the phrasing and priorities seemed today, the Pole had established standards, and expectations still followed, even as the discipline minced to the latest fashions of scholarship. One of the text's precepts, novel at the time, was that ethnographers actually live with the people they study.

So what do you think? he asked no one in particular.

Boring, said the voice.

Heads bobbed.

What was boring about it?

It was repetitive.

Yeah, said another, with a mousy goatee and a large knit ski cap over long matted hair, legs spread wide and loose, hiking boots like luggage at his feet. He went on and on about the smallest things.

But don't the details help? he asked. Don't they reassure you that he was there, knew those things?

More coffee?

Thanks.

Oatmeal's on its way.

Thanks.

Yeah, well, he's still boring, said the voice.

That's not a substantive criticism. The guy's been read by everyone in the field, and most find what he has to say important. To dismiss him simply because you find him boring isn't reasonable.

But it's true.

You're just banging him to bang him. Walk in his shoes for a while. He's asking you to see the world from another's point of view. That's hard. It's the hardest thing you'll ever do. It's not enough to be smart. You have to give up part of yourself.

But you really can't do that, can you?

It was a young woman who rarely spoke.

How do we know he hasn't had some effect on them just being there? she said. Maybe he's changed them.

It was a question that came up. The observer effect. The uncertainty principle. He was never sure how to answer it.

Of course, he's going to have some effect, he said. But how much? What sort of effect would a stranger have on your life? Let's not give him too much credit. He was just a solitary academic with a tent and a typewriter.

They laughed at this and looked at each other.

Here you go. The woman in the smock was back with the oatmeal.

Anything else?

Thanks, I'm fine.

Sure?

Yeah, I'm OK. Thanks.

He sprinkled sugar on the steaming oatmeal, added milk, and stirred, continuing to think about the class.

But he had power, didn't he? It was the one with the goatee. He was with the colonials. We've been talking about globalization in another class. Isn't that how it happens? People from one side show up. Maybe they're tourists. Maybe they're anthropologists. Maybe they're Walmart. They can't help but pass on values. Isn't that corrupting? I mean, maybe they like the guy and all. Maybe he learns their language. They like having him around. But they're never going to be the same again.

You're right, he said. We change people. They change us. Welcome to the world. We change each other. We damage each other. It's also how we learn. What's the alternative? Give it up? No contact? Maybe we shouldn't try.

The students looked at their notebooks.

Maybe we shouldn't, said the goatee, who was braver than the rest. The world would be better off if people minded their own business.

There followed a beat of silence.

It was an anthropology class. What if its practitioners minded their own business?

He wondered what she would have said.

The students waited.

You've got dreads, right? he said. Those come from Africa by way of Jamaica. But you're a white guy. Those dreads aren't part of your history. Do you feel damaged?

He didn't like to put students on the spot that way, encroach on them, but there it was in the room.

That's different, said the goatee. I chose my locks. Nobody made me do my hair this way.

So couldn't the Trobriand Islanders pick and choose what they wanted from the anthropologist? Perhaps there were things they liked, wanted to imitate, wanted to wear.

How free were they to choose whether he was there in the first place? It was the voice, chiming in with the right question. And even if they were, he's still writing about *their* traditions, not his—how does he *know* what's theirs and what they've learned from him or others?

Wouldn't it be better, she went on, if they wrote their own stories? The only people to get their names in these books are anthropologists. The people themselves—the individuals, I mean—are nameless. Turn that around. Give them back their names.

That's a good idea, he said. But you still have the problem of point of view. It shifts. But it doesn't go away.

The difference, she said, is that he's presenting his views as their views, even though they're really just his thoughts. How do we know he's learned *their* point of view? It just doesn't seem very likely. Like he's claiming to know what Martians think.

Except, he said, he didn't live with Martians. He lived with these people. How do any of you know what anyone thinks, even in your own society? How do I know what you mean?

We speak the same language, objected one who'd been listening until now.

And how did we come to speak that language?

Growing up in the same place, I guess.

The voice now drew the conversation back.

Obviously it's possible to communicate meanings, she said, arms crossed impatiently, right leg bobbing over left. I mean, none of us doubts he moved from Poland to England and got along OK. He became head of that school. Why couldn't he go to New Guinea, or wherever?

The issue, she continued, is his privilege to be there in the first place. It's not like those people get to come here. Our immigration laws make that difficult. But we get to go anywhere we want, do what we like, spread our values around the world.

The goatee lifted his hand for a change.

It's not just culture, either. What about disease? What if he introduces some disease that they don't have? I mean, that actually happened, right? The first colonizers brought diseases that decimated indigenous populations. That could happen again, couldn't it?

Another voice chimed in, emboldened by the critical turn: I read a book about that. An anthropologist exposed some Amazonian Indians to smallpox or measles or something, supposedly to test their immune systems, their biological fitness …

He'd let the conversation drift.

He wasn't sure how to bring it back. He shared their outrage that anyone would set out intentionally to harm others. But just because people hurt each other wasn't reason to stop associating. Was it? It would have been easy enough to say, but he couldn't find the words. All of a sudden he had no patience. People around the world were blowing each other up. People who didn't even want to know about each other. These kids, safe in their classroom, worried about the influence a few anthropologists had on the folks they studied.

He shrugged his shoulders.

Of course it's wrong to harm others, he said. But should we stop trying to understand each other because sometimes we screw up? What kind of a world would that be?

They nodded their heads. But they weren't convinced. They were skeptical as ever.

They thought anthropology was a science. Its practitioners weren't supposed to affect the subjects of their investigations. The fact anthropologists actually lived with people they studied, and in that way touched them, changed them, seemed unscientific. It was subjective. In their minds that made a lie of the whole works.

Perhaps they were right.

He felt like a lie.

A shell in a shell game. Hiding a pea.

On the way back to his office, he stopped to check his mailbox and found the blue aérogramme.

Everything all right?

The woman in the rolled sleeves startled him. She picked up the empty bowl.

Fine, he said. Fine. Thanks.

No problem. More coffee?

No. Just the check.

He was committed to few things, had no political agenda, did not pretend to understand the world's problems. He was pragmatic enough to know that compromise was necessary. But how far and in which direction? He didn't know. There was only one thing he believed: Avoid doing harm. He'd held the idea throughout. But without meaning to, he'd hurt the last person in the world he'd have ever wanted to hurt, the one he loved.

It was the same with medicine. Think of the people doctors harmed as they tried to help.

He paid his check at the counter. His flight was tonight, and he needed his passport stamped with a visa. The travel agent had assured him it was sent express and would arrive by noon today. She'd given him the tracking number. The number reassured him. It was in his wallet. He'd called, and they'd said it had arrived and would be delivered today.

That was science.

The news in the priest's letter was something else.

PRAYERS ARE COMMON *in Dasse life, but Dasse do not pray at burials. Nor do they pray at the ceremonies immediately after. In fact, the surviving family may not pray until after* sorio hamtu, *a sacrifice up to a year later that marks the end of* hamtu, *the time of mourning. During* hamtu *the dead man's sons, brothers, and grandsons may not cut their hair or beards, clip the nails of their fingers or toes, participate in feasts, brand or clip the ears of livestock, or castrate male livestock. A dead man's surviving wife may not cook inside her tent, and his wife, unmarried daughters, and daughters-in-law may not oil their hair. They hold themselves outside formal practices, in a state of suspended animation, until their mourning has ended, when they reenter ordinary life. Though there is undoubted grief, there is no period of* hamtu *following a woman's death.*

XVI

In the days leading up to his return, he had not slept at home. The house had ceased to be a comfort. He camped instead at a friend's, slept on a soft couch in the study, and slept poorly. He was exhausted. The semester was over. Grades were in. His flight was that night. He hadn't packed. He'd walked to the diner, and now he walked to the house. It was only half a mile, through an old neighborhood that had gone, in one generation, from white working class to black working class and back to white, but not working class—upmarket, professional. Huge oaks and hemlocks haunted the streets. Their roots pitched and rolled the sidewalks. The power company had lopped off the tops of the trees along the road, and they stood betopped, blunted, like a child's drawing of trees. The houses were all about a hundred years old, made of cedar shakes and stucco and stone. Most were bungalows with wide shady porches and gabled attics and stone walls on the edges of small lawns. Many flew a signature flag by the front door. The windows above the doors were made of stained glass. Modernist sculptures, abstract figures with rough organic shapes and surfaces, had sprouted in gardens. Only a few of the old houses remained empty, yet to be captured by so-called urban pioneers.

Snow had begun to fall while he was eating breakfast, and he walked through a gauze of wispy powder. There was less than an inch on the ground. Blades of grass stuck through the whiteness like fingertips in open-fingered gloves. Snow caught on the tops of the bare black branches and drew them into relief. Wind blew dusty swirls across the pavement. He thought of desert sand blowing across the surface of dunes.

He'd grown up in a village of deep snows. The town consisted of houses on a cross-hatching of tree-lined streets flanking a crossroads. A drugstore with a soda fountain stood on one corner, a hardware store with wood floors and high ceilings on another, the town hall on a third. He couldn't remember what was on the fourth. A lawyer's office, perhaps. From hooks in the ceiling of the butcher shop hung pieces of meat that resembled the animals they'd been. All they lacked was skin. The butcher had a glass jar, big as a beer keg, full of the largest pickles he'd ever seen. They were a nickel each. There was a grocery store on the main road a couple of doors down from the drugstore. The stores were always open, even if it snowed three feet in the night. His mother told him the owners lived above. He remembered walking to town, pulling a sled, a toy rifle over his shoulder, scouting Indians.

Walking now in the snow along the street in his own neighborhood, he thought of the glass paperweights he liked as a child. They were heavy and fluid-filled and contained whole winter scenes—an Alpine chalet, say—and if you shook the glass, snow fell as it was falling now. When he was a kid the glass ball was a winter fantasy incarnate: He always wished he could enter the ball, go to that place, despite its similarity to his own place in winter. The fact it was sealed off and unchanging but for the falling snow was what appealed to him. The fantasy in the ball represented a fixed place somewhere else. Now this reality, here on the street by his house, represented the childhood fantasy. Wherever you were, he thought, you were elsewhere. He drew his hand through his hatless hair and combed wet snow into the grooves of his fingers.

His footsteps slowed as he neared. He approached from behind, along a side street, and he could see the backyard through hedges and falling snow.

He was drawn by the house, pulled by a force that managed, like two magnets against each other, to repel at the same time. So though he was excited to be home, he was not eager to go inside. He would go in. He had to batten the place for the time he'd be away. He needed things to take with him: his traveling pack, some clothes. He did not think of what else he needed to do there, and this was like him, for he seldom thought of feelings until they were upon him, and then he had no choice but to cope as best he could, without premeditation.

The house was closed, blinds shut. It looked asleep, snow falling all around, deepening. Smoke rose from the chimneys of other houses on the street, but this one stood still and dark. His were the first footprints up the sidewalk to the door. He stopped on the porch and banged his shoes against the wall to shake off the snow. Only then did he reach into his pocket for the keys.

The house was cold. The air was stale, like air in a closet. He opened the curtains and blinds at the front.

The lines, angles, and shadows were all so familiar that he expected a voice to call from the back: Is that you? He resisted an urge to answer.

The exchange was a habit learned from years of living together. When she returned she'd call into the house, whether he was there or not, on the odds he was: Honey, I'm home. He'd hear the groan of the door opening, the sigh of it closing. He knew she was home. She liked him to announce himself from the door as well, and he used to think it was because she didn't hear the door. Several times he had startled her, walking into a back room where she was reading, appearing like that, intruder or ghost. Her ears were fine; she concentrated so hard she didn't hear noises. It was the custom in her house growing up to call out a greeting at the door. Her father had done it when he came home from work, and her mother when she returned from a meeting or the grocery store. He did it to suit her, and it became a habit: Honey, I'm home. She would answer from the back room, Hey, babe. How are you? The greetings, like a matched set, like bookends, met each other, clasped, filled the place. He did not call now, and not calling made him think of her more than if he had called. Her absence made her as much of a presence as when she was here, for the whole house groaned without her.

He put the accumulated mail on the dining room table and dropped his coat onto a chair. He did not look through the mail. Anything he wanted, except bills, went to the university. He made a mental note to pay the bills. He thought he should write down these notes he made to himself, that otherwise they were lost as soon as he turned his attention to something else. But he did not write it down. He did not walk into the back room, either, but turned in the hallway and went to the basement to get his bag.

The basement was darker than upstairs, despite its open, uncurtained windows. The basement was only partly underground. In the back it stood fully above ground, and a door and windows led out to the side. The garden and carpentry tools lay still and disorganized on shelves and benches, their glints dulled by the dust and the bruised light from the sky outside, like artifacts of a shipwreck in dark and silty waters.

The other half of the basement was her studio. He did not go there.

The bag was covered with dust, and he shook it—once, again, and again—surrounding himself in a cloud that made him sneeze and took a long time to settle in the chilly stillness. He stood for a while and looked at the tools in the light coming through the window. He scraped the concrete floor with his foot to make a noise. The snow outside made no noise and absorbed outside noises. No one waited upstairs. He had no one to meet, nowhere to go, not until tonight, and the fact made him weary. He did not really want to pack, though he knew it would take him no time at all. How long would it take to throw a change of clothing, a book, a toothbrush, a memory into a satchel?

He climbed the steps and, avoiding the bedroom, went back through the hallway to the dining room, kicked off his shoes, which would scuff the kitchen floor, and from there stepped into the kitchen. The bowl and cup from his breakfast five days before were still in the sink. The last of the coffee stood cold and tarry in the glass beaker. He'd left the milk out. He smelled it and it was OK. The house had been cold. He put the carton back in the refrigerator. He might not have been gone at all. He washed the dishes, wiped the counter, sopping up the spilled water and suds. He filled a kettle with water and set it on the stove to boil.

He looked out the window. The bird feeders were empty. He was bad about filling them. She had always done it, and throughout the illness he'd kept them full so she could see the birds from the bed in the back room beside the kitchen. Then he'd forgotten the birds. They were her birds. He'd liked them well enough, but not enough to think to feed them. Now he went back to the basement and got the sack of birdseed from a plastic container and carried it to the porch and filled the containers. Black sunflower seeds. The birds rejected all else.

They liked sunflowers. He gave them sunflowers.

The water boiled. He made the tea and carried it into the bedroom. He sat in the Shaker chair they'd bought together and sipped the tea. He thought to tell her about Abudo and smiled. If she could hear she already knew. Perhaps they are together, he thought, then rubbed his face to wipe away the thought. He looked at the bed. There were small depressions where their bodies had lain, scallops in the duff of the surface. He set his tea on the night table and crawled into the bed.

He lay on his side, facing her, wanting to reach out across the space between them, to feel her weight against his, like bookends.

And he slept.

FOR MEN WITH *responsibilities, the mourning period of* hamtu *is inconvenient. I knew a man, Diba Ali, the* abba magalata *of Olla Yaa Galbo, whose brother died, which meant Diba had* hamtu. *The* abba magalata *keeps the* magalata, *a ceremonial horn made of a hollowed elephant's tusk, fringed with long strips of skin from sacrificed bulls. At all important occasions, such as after the sighting of a new moon or when the camp is to move, the* abba magalata *blows the horn. There is no attempt at melody, just long successive blasts. Because of* hamtu, *Diba could not blow the horn. The brother had lived in a camp twelve miles distant, and Diba was now spending much of his time there. His absence made it difficult for elders in his own camp to decide what to do. There was talk of appointing a new* abba magalata, *which would have embarrassed Diba and his family. In the end, they asked his firstborn son, who did not have* hamtu, *to blow the horn.*

XVII

The present

He sat before Elema's tent and watched Ado. She reminded him of a dryland antelope called a gerenuk, which had the long neck and body of a ballerina. The gerenuk was a ballerina, up on its toes, reaching into the acacia bush. It never ran but leapt. Ado's neck was long. She held her head up to show it. Her hair was not plaited like the other women, as she was still in mourning and her hair had not grown out enough since Abudo's death when she had shaved it. There was a wide gap, like a keyhole, between her front teeth, which in his world was unremarkable but here was loveliness itself. She had creamy smooth skin and dark intelligent eyes, and she smiled in the easy way of someone profoundly amused by life. He liked her smile.

Back home people might have thought her behavior was bawdy, but here it was not bawdy so much as the mature manner of a woman.

It was not sexual, not in any simple way. It imposed distance between herself and others, suggested confidence and superiority. She took orders easily from no one—not now, not when Abudo was alive. She'd been Abudo's partner, not his servant. He remembered that from before.

One day, only a few months into his fieldwork, when he was just starting to get to know Abudo, hardly had any language skills, was traveling with an assistant, a translator, a boy named Charfi from the Catholic school in Maikona, he arrived for a visit. Abudo's camp was then pitched within a two-hour walk of Maikona, and he had made a day of it, arriving in late morning across the dusty lunar landscape.

Abudo invited him into the tent. The tent was technically Ado's. He knew that. Wives alone owned tents, not husbands. They got them at marriage, added parts and increased their size as their families matured, and then gave away parts to marrying female relatives until, late in life, when they were old widows, they had little more than a lean-to for shelter, their husbands long dead, their daughters with tents of their own, their sons with wives of their own.

Husbands tended to behave as if they owned the tents.

Abudo had been resting in the back. He asked Ado to make tea for their guest.

She looked the guest over with an appraising smile. She said there was no firewood.

Abudo said, It's just there. You fetched it this morning.

She said there was no milk.

Abudo said, It's there. We have not drunk the milk from today.

That, she said, I'm saving for my boyfriend.

She used the masculine gender for a term that literally meant my friend, *jal kiya*.

Charfi, the assistant, who'd been translating, smiled awkwardly.

It was an unusual tack to take with a husband. Wives had lovers just as husbands did, but they did not, as a rule, talk about them with each other.

Ado's smile, however, indicated she was teasing.

Abudo smiled, too.

Well then, Abudo said to Ado, it's good you saved it, for he seems to have arrived.

Ado smiled, stuck out her tongue at Abudo, then looked at the guest. It seems I will need milk for both of you.

She turned back to Abudo: I promised your brother's wife that I would help her with firewood.

The visitor did not know how to respond. He answered her reluctance to make tea: *Yaquf'*, he said. I'm full and have no room for tea.

There, you see, she said. The guest is satisfied. And with that she left.

Abudo smiled broadly.

The guest was not sure whether Abudo was putting on a face to hide an irritation or was really amused. It was hard to tell.

Abudo took the opportunity to give him a language lesson. He told the assistant to listen carefully as well, that he also might learn something. Charfi came from a settled family in town, had never lived in a tent, did not know much about nomadic life.

Abudo lay on his wife's bed on the south side of the tent. The other two sat on Abudo's bed. Abudo parted a section of matting at the rear, opened for ventilation but also to let in light. He pointed at different objects, said their names, and asked him to repeat, returning to ones he'd already identified to test his memory.

Cup, sack, fire sticks, knife, oil container, coffee bowl, tobacco sack, cloth, cup, water container, shoe, knife, butter churn, milk container, coffee bowl, cloth, and so on.

He enjoyed the attention, enjoyed Abudo's enthusiasm for giving him a lesson, but he also felt a little foolish, like a child being taught a simple lesson by an amused father. He was aware then, for the first time, that he was at least as old as Abudo, maybe older, yet Abudo regarded him in this sense as a child. He took only a little comfort from the fact Charfi, a boy from town, did not know many of the objects either.

Half an hour later, Ado drew the tent flaps open. They had not heard her coming. The new light flooded the tent. She looked in and smiled.

Wait, she said.

She returned with a large cup, holding a pint of rich milky tea, and handed it to the guest.

For my friend, she said, smiling all the while at Abudo.

She left and in a moment returned from Elema's wife's tent with two more cups, equally large, for Abudo and Charfi.

Now, so many years later, he sat in front of Elema's tent and watched Ado, and the thought of her made him think of his wife.

⁂

He woke in the gray dawn, before the others, and picked his way among the rocks into the bush where he would relieve his bowels, which was, with all the milk he was drinking, increasingly difficult. He returned to camp, by which time women were stoking fires. He could hear the cracking of branches inside tents and see the gray smoke lifting off the tents like steam. Stone mounds stood like sentinels beside the corrals for the goats and sheep. They were waist high, the size of large trash cans. They looked like small graves. When he had first visited Dasse camps he assumed they were piles of rocks cleared for the tents and corrals. So he was surprised, walking past one of these cairns one day, to hear the bleating of lambs coming from within. They were, he discovered, not piles at all, but shelters, stone igloos. A large flat stone on top served as the lid. They were ingenious shelters: They provided protection and shade for lambs and kids, which were not much bigger than large rabbits and easily borne away by predators. Here they remained all night and much of the day, pulled out by their necks to suckle their mothers' teats and to graze for part of the day under the distracted gaze of children.

As he sat now outside Elema's tent he could see the slit-eyed kids watching from within, between the cracks, bleating for their mothers, bleating for their lives.

Elema emerged from the tent, sleep in his eyes, coughing from smoke, clearing his throat.

There was no doubt Elema was Abudo's brother.

They might have been twins. Same complexion. Same hair. Same mouth, same nose. Different eyes. The tuft of hair that grew on Elema's chin and nowhere else on his face was longer than Abudo's. Because he was still in mourning, Elema's hair and fingernails were long, wild looking, but his dishevelment gave him a kind of grace. He'd always thought Abudo and Elema looked like characters from *The Arabian Nights*, windblown, hard as tree bark. Abudo in particular had been sharp and well defined—when he moved you could see every muscle roll into the next as if stretched by a taffy machine. Elema was softer and heavier. Not in flesh; he was no larger than Abudo. But he was weighted, lumberish, slow. When you talked to Abudo, he leaned in close and listened and nodded his head and pursed his lips. You were the only one. He asked questions. Elema started a conversation with questions and listened but asked no more and soon lost interest.

Seeing Elema made him want Abudo all the more.

They sat without speaking and stared at the goats and sheep, which panted like tired dogs in the corral, weary of harassing each other all night. Billy goats and rams troubled the dams endlessly. They wore themselves out. He'd read somewhere that males did not live long because they worked at sex all the time, seldom rested, hardly ate enough, rarely let themselves be distracted from the task of fighting off other males and squirting semen into as many females as they could mount. Depending on how one thought about such things, the males had it pretty good: They roved the pen like autograph hounds at a movie premiere. No sooner had they dismounted one female than they sniffed out another.

Elema's wife handed them tea. There was milk in camp. Leaves had not yet blossomed on the bushes, but there was more water, and at least for the time being camels' milk was flowing more plentifully than before. Spirits had eased after the rain. The fact the rains did not continue, however, was refueling anxieties. Men were spending more time huddled up discussing places to which the camp might move—greener places, where it might have rained more or where they might go should the rains stop altogether. Several had already left with older sons to scout new pastures. Some wanted to move farther north, across the national border, nearer the escarpment to the northern highlands. It was likely to have rained more there.

Still, for the time being, life in camp was easier than it had been. Women did not have to take loading camels to haul water from the wells so far away. They were getting water from the *lagga* and would for at least another week.

He read the books he brought. He waited.

The old social thinkers called what he suffered *anomie*, which, if you broke it down, meant without order or perhaps without name, which in any case amounted to the same thing. What he wanted remained unnamed, unsaid, because he didn't know what to say, and even if he did, he wouldn't know how. But it wasn't bad. It wasn't depression. He was waiting. And waiting was what pastoralists did almost all the time. They were nothing if not patient: waiting on animals to eat, waiting on them to drink, waiting on them as they walked back to pasture. Even when they were trekking fifty miles in a single day they were waiting, waiting to get there. Studying them had largely been a matter of waiting with them, letting them decide when it was time to talk and what to talk about. He got nowhere hurrying.

⁂

He shifted his time and attention from Elema to Ado. It was not conscious. He simply drifted into her orbit, though they said little to each other. He sat there in the morning, and she brought him tea from Elema's tent, where she did her cooking, since she, too, was in mourning. One night he was resting beside her tent, chewing tobacco, watching the night sky, speaking now and then with Elema across the way, and Elema's son brought him the cow skin to lie on. After that he slept beside Ado's tent, she inside.

He told himself it was not Ado but Abudo that drew him there. Between them he felt an intimacy without words, without understanding, just proximity.

⁂

The silence woke him. The sheep and goats were quiet. It was as if they'd all died. He raised his head. Small stock were never quiet, not even in the middle of the night, not en masse. Everything was at rest. Even the air was still. He could hear Ali breathing deeply over by Elema's tent.

He lay his head down and turned on his back and looked up at the black cloud forms against the stars. He remembered that the wind often slowed or stopped in the middle of the night before it started up again an hour or so before dawn. It was the same midday. He thought it had to do with being far, in the earth's rotation, from the edge of light and dark.

The silence must have disturbed the dogs. Elema's mutt was standing in front of the tent, looking into the darkness. Something scurried beyond the pens. Rustle of dry branches. Clatter of rocks. The dog whined. Then growled. He raised his head again but could see nothing over the brush. The dog stood and barked, was joined immediately by a chorus of others in the camp, and disappeared into the dark.

At almost the same time, so he wasn't sure whether they'd been provoked by the dogs barking or something else, the goats and sheep in the pens began to scream and bawl. Their noise was the noise of a traffic jam, everyone honking like the others, no one sure why. The flock jumped and pressed against the thorn-branch walls of the enclosure. They clamored against the near walls. Whatever they sought to avoid was on the far side.

Over the din of dogs and sheep and goats, he heard another, more certain sound. It was not a sound reacting to other sounds. It was its own sound, made for its own reasons. A loud whoop, like the blast of a police siren, both mournful and frightening. The whoop was followed by sharp coughs.

He stood but was unsure what to do. He pulled on his sandals and crawled into his shirt. He heard others inside tents. Ado's daughter whimpered. Ado whispered.

Ali stirred beside Elema's tent.

Hyenas were attacking the sheep.

He had seen hyenas plenty of times but never menacing a herd. He knew the threat they posed to the livestock. He was not afraid, not for himself. The hyenas were after the stock, not humans. But they were opportunists. He was horrified and enthralled. He remembered a film on hyenas he'd seen long ago. The narrator said hyenas were masters of confusion. That was their strategy. Create chaos, then grab what they could in their massive jaws and carry it off.

Elema stumbled from the tent.

The hyenas seemed to be concentrating their efforts here, on the northern end of camp. He could hear rocks tumble and whoops and the press of frightened bodies against the thorn branches of Elema's *boma* and others nearby. There must have been half a dozen hyenas.

Warabesa, he told Elema needlessly.

Elema grabbed his spear and shouted alarm. He ran out along the edge of the corral. Ali rose, pulling on his sandals, and stood. A boy he knew in camp called for him, and Ali ran toward the voice. Others emerged from tents. Ado came out to see and stood, holding her daughter. He followed Elema, tentatively, with more curiosity than purpose, fearful of hurting himself on the rocks, eager to watch. Men and women shouted. They ran forward into the darkness. Words rang out amid the alarm.

Mirga! Mirga! North! North!

That way!

Here!

Ay, ay, ay!

He shouted as well but did not know why he was shouting and quit.

He wanted to watch. He was an anthropologist, after all. His job had always been to observe, document, record. Like a journalist at a riot. Which side was he on? Stone the journalist, he thought. He blamed himself for thinking too much. But it was what he knew to do. He didn't want to blunder into a hyena and be attacked. He didn't want to drive one the wrong way. He wanted to be helpful, effective, not just make noise. And he didn't know how. He knew only to be there.

He followed Elema, who dashed one way and then another, pursuing hyenas that gave ground only to sneak back again. Someone clicked on a flashlight and panned it over the scene. He saw at least three hyenas but knew from the noise that there must be more. Other flashlights farther south in the camp snicked the air like shooting stars. They made everything darker.

Several hyenas galloped away, their big shoulders and small flanks making an awkward sideways shamble, looking over their shoulders, retreating into the night.

One had a goat in its mouth, light as a cookie.

A flashlight followed.

Everything else was darkness washed in the faintest light of stars.

The camp was built beside *bulle*, what was once, a million years ago, a wave of lava that had frozen and cracked and was now a ridge of dark boulders that ran east-west just north of camp. At the end of camp, there were no more than twenty feet between the outer edge of the corrals and the foot of the boulders.

He rounded Elema's corral, waving his arms, shouting, adding a body to the defense. He saw bear-like shadows in the near distance. They did not move as a pack but in every which direction. Some scurried south, others north, several retreated, a few charged. They were children playing tag: Chase one, and the rest were free to scatter where they wanted. Who knew how to organize a defense against such confusion?

A small group of men and women rushed around on the north side of camp, beyond the last corral that way, and hyenas that didn't make it through were chased south. Here they were headed off by Elema and others, he among them.

The boulders rose as a cliff, black against the sky, and beneath it he could see almost nothing.

In front of this black scrim there was a movement, a darkness against darkness, trapped between phalanxes of rushing men and women with waving arms. Shadows on shadows. None of it clear. Except a sound. The hyena giggled. Was it nervous? Was it calling for help? Was it going to charge? What could you make of such a sound from such an animal? For a moment, no one seemed to know what to do, whether to throw spears and stones and risk missing, risk its escape.

Then came a cry from behind.

A man's cry. A wail.

Out of the star fog a large man lunged, spear raised. He rushed between them through darkness toward darkness. He did not pause. He did not seem to touch the ground. He moved as a sprinter, an athlete, a javelin thrower, knees high and forward, feet back, spine erect, right arm raised with spear. He dropped his arm forward as he neared the hulking form and in one unwavering motion plunged the spear into the hyena before it had any sense of what was happening.

The cry silenced the others.

The other hyenas paused, then retreated. The shadows withdrew.

The entire drama had lasted a couple of minutes only.

A flashlight approached, dandled like a lit cigarette against the night. The dead hyena lay, spear plunged into its mouth, spread-legged on the ground. The muscles of its flanks quivered. The black eyes stared at everything and nothing. The face was frightening, the ghost of a pit bull, a figure from a horror film.

The people thought it was horror itself.

They stood and looked at it. Someone prodded the body with a spear. To test its death. To gauge its heft. It seemed now small and insignificant. Another man with a staff joined the man with the spear, and together they turned the beast on its side. It had a round puppy's belly. It had a black penis, like a long foreskin. The man with the stick touched the hyena's penis. Elema frowned in the harsh light of the flashlight. He said it looked male but was not male or female. Hyenas, he said, were both.

Hamtu, he said. Evil.

The female spotted hyena, common on the desert, had what biologists called masculinized genitalia. He'd read about that. Females had large amounts of the male hormone testosterone in their blood. In a place like this, among these masters of confusion, females benefited from being aggressive, even more aggressive than males. Evolution had favored those with high levels of testosterone. In a mob of spotted hyenas, one female dominated the others. She was largest. She was the matriarch. She would bear the most offspring, out through her penis, and they would share her status.

He knew hyenas were bad because they killed livestock. But he did not fully understand Elema's repugnance. For Elema, it was not simply that hyenas killed livestock. Humans stole and killed livestock, but Elema did not think they personified evil.

He had asked about this. Dasse told him hyenas lacked clarity. They were unnatural. He pointed out that Waaqa, their divinity, was also both male and female, and Waaqa was surely not evil. They said that was different. Waaqa created everything so partook of everything. *Warabesa* destroyed everything and that's why they were mixed up.

The man who killed the hyena withdrew his spear and scraped the blood from it on a stone. He was a visitor to camp, having come, like him, for *imaltu*, to request a favor from a friend or relative. He thought the other man would probably get what he asked for.

They left the body—not wanting to touch it, hoping the other hyenas would drag it away and eat it—and returned to the tents. Perhaps it would serve as a warning. Several men checked their corrals. They'd lost some goats and sheep. They'd count in the morning. Men and women alike were full of the noise of congratulation and relief, retelling what had happened, shaping the chaos into a story that they would remember.

Women reentered their tents.

Ado went inside, whispering her daughter's name.

Ali was off with others his age.

He lay on the skin beside Ado's tent and listened as men talked in front of their tents.

Elema called his name.

Eh, he responded.

You have seen something tonight, Elema said. Have you seen how it is? Have you seen how we suffer?

Elema asked again if he had seen, told him that was how to kill *warabesa*, that he should write that down. People would find something like that interesting.

Eh, he agreed.

Elema resumed his conversation with the other man. Their talk faded to whispers, and soon each returned to his bed and slept. Somewhere a baby cried but quickly found its mother's breast and stopped.

He lay on his back and looked at the sky and what he could see, where there were no clouds, of the Milky Way, and he remembered what Dasse called the Milky Way: *Kara Warabesa*, the Hyena's Path. It lit the sky like phosphorous from horizon to horizon. Legend was a hyena had killed its own mother and dragged the body away, creating a path in the stars like a carcass dragged across pebbles.

He had not helped kill the hyena.

But then few of them had done much more than run around and shout and raise their arms in the sky. They'd met confusion with confusion. Only the one man, a stranger, had known when to strike and with what acute force, cutting through the chaos with a single, dedicated purpose, not trying to drive them all away or even to protect the animals but to kill this one, and only this one.

SORIO HAMTU, THE *sacrifice to end mourning, must occur in one of three propitious months within the twelve-month lunar calendar: Soom D'era, Soom D'era Egi, or Yaqaa. The two Soom D'era fall next to each other; Yaqaa occurs five months later. They are months for sacrifices, weddings, and circumcisions, as well as for trading camels, beginning to train camels, and branding camels. The three months are called* jia gaala, *or camel months.* Sorio hamtu *occurs about a year after the death.*

XVIII

Weeks before

He showed his passport, shouldered the small rucksack, and stepped into the long corridor. The old, oil-stained bag contained a notebook and a couple of pens, a change of underwear, a shirt, a pair of khaki shorts, a pair of sandals made of old tires, a toothbrush and razor, a light sweater, a bottle of water. He watched others straining with carry-on bags that stretched the definition. He enjoyed traveling light, was smug about it. He had no suitcase. No checked baggage. If he needed something, he'd buy it. For the moment there were no attachments. Nothing but the sense of civility that connected him to and liberated him from everyone else in the airports he would float through over the next twenty-four hours. No one else knew quite where he was, except perhaps the travel agent, and she was just a voice on the phone. He was alone, yet people flowed all around, pulsing to rhythms set by the television screens mounted on concourse walls. He never felt freer than when he was traveling like this—never safer, more confined, more like the tiniest unit in a larger organism whose aims and direction were beyond his grasp, and his beyond its.

He flew into the capital, arriving in the morning. He dodged a field of baggage dollies on his way to the customs counters. There he was assumed—given the satchel over his shoulder, the informality of his clothing, the color of his skin—to be a tourist and waved through. He walked past the crowd waiting to collect loved ones, clients, and guests. Some carried signs with names on them. No one had come to meet him.

He accepted the first taxi, haggling briefly over the fare, which had doubled in the intervening years. The taxi carried him into the city, past towering palms and hunched marabou storks, blank-eyed as undertakers. The cab dropped him at the Flora Hostel, a walled convent on a hill of aging tile-roofed estates outside the city center. The neighborhood was shaded by tall eucalyptus trees. Black kites, sleek as swallows, patrolled the air above the treetops. Punk fires smoldered in yards and gardens. They gave the equatorial air the odor of autumn. He remembered raking leaves as a boy with his father and brother, and burning them afterward, how slowly they burned, more smoke than flame.

The hostel was quiet. He liked that. The room contained a narrow bed, a table, a chair, a small sink, a wardrobe, a crucifix on the wall. A window opened to a shaded yard with a huge fig tree and a hedge of bougainvillea. He considered staying a few days and resting but rejected the idea. This was not the time to rest.

He left the hostel and walked downtown and bought a bus ticket to the end of the northern line. It was less than half as far as he would go. He could have taken a missionary plane all the way—he had the money—but he liked the idea of making the journey as before, seeing the country through. He returned to the hostel for lunch, then walked to the university. No one he knew was in. No one expected him. A shy, round-faced secretary behind a desk told him that the professor he asked for—a middle-aged man with bushy hair, large smile, and gapped front teeth—had died. How? He was ill. So young, he said. She shrugged her shoulders. She would say no more. Another member of the faculty he mentioned had retired since he had been away. She didn't know where he was. She did not offer to find out. He drifted among the books in the library, but they did not interest him. Even the journals were old. Students sat at tables in window light, piles of books at their elbows, writing on loose-leaf paper the color and texture of newsprint.

He walked through the city, looking in windows, enjoying the anonymity. He played a game as he went, finding words on signs that began with succeeding letters of the alphabet. It was a sort of walking solitaire. He tried to remember the words in order, but there were too many distractions and most of the words were in the national language and hard to memorize. He noticed his reflection in the window of a shoe store, saw a gaunt unshaven face above an oversized white shirt and wrinkled khaki trousers. He was a bone of his former self, tented within the loose cotton clothing. He turned away. He watched the crowds on the street. He dodged traffic, moved with the capillary flow of pedestrians, avoided the eyes of gas-sniffing street boys. He handed change to a beggar woman who sat against a wall with a baby. Her legs, stretched out in front of her, ended at ankles without feet. He stopped at a clothing shop and bought another pair of cotton shorts, T-shirts, a package of underwear, and a green canvas hat with a wide brim against the sun. Outside, he bought a newspaper and an armful of used paperbacks from a sidewalk vendor, who called him *mzee*, old man. The word startled him. He stopped at a café to drink a cup of coffee. In the evening he returned to the hostel, ate a light supper, went to his room, and, with the help of a tablet, slept.

He rose early, before light, took a cab to the bus station, and rode the crowded bus north out of the city.

The bus passed farms with gardens cleared in hopes of rain. He watched men plowing fields with oxen, sweaty skin glistening in the warm sunlight. The dry red dirt scarred the green land. Banana trees stood beside earthen houses, big leaves wagging like elephant ears in the wind. Women with buckets of water balanced on their heads stepped along the narrow pathways with the practiced ease of dancers. Others nearer the road, walking to market with heavy sacks of produce on their backs, became a blur to the rushing bus.

All morning they climbed. The cool, alpine air was bright with sun. The driver slowed for markets, packed with people and taxis and piles of fruits and vegetables and cheap brightly colored plastic wares and young boys selling sodas and cigarettes. They sped past farms with thatched or rusted iron-sheet roofs and children playing in carefully swept clay yards. Faces and costumes changed as they rolled north, letting off passengers, picking up others. People got thinner, less friendly, more familiar to him. The bus passed highland pastures, undulating brown hummocks and swales. These looked like home. The bus crossed the equator. A sign said so. A mountain there, high enough to wear a crown of ice and snow, buried its craggy, oyster-shell summit in clouds the color of tidewater. They had once climbed the mountain. When they were young. Late that afternoon, the bus descended through rolling country onto a sandy plain, and as dusk fell, the yellow sand dimmed to darkness.

⁂

That evening he checked into a hotel for traders and businessmen made of rough concrete and rebar and glass windows set into metal frames. Shelf paper lay on the floor in lieu of tile. It was clean and quiet. In the dark morning he was wakened by the muezzin. He rose and showered and walked to a row of lorries at the edge of town waiting to make the journey north over an endless dirt road. The police would not allow drivers to move at night because of bandits. There were no buses beyond here. The lorries were diesel trucks with huge, tarpaulin-covered loads upon which drivers carried passengers for extra cash. It was like riding on top of a boat. He picked one that looked somewhat well maintained, as if it would make the journey over the deeply rutted road. He was no mechanic. He just guessed. The driver knocked the charge down when he argued about it in the northern language. It was all under ten dollars. It wasn't the money. He simply wanted the driver to know he wasn't here for the scenery.

The lorry had a flat on the way.

Then another.

Each time, he dropped to the road with the others and pissed on the side with the sun and then joined the rest in the shade. He squinted over the dry, stone-strewn land. There was no wildlife. In the afternoon, even the crows settled into what shade they could find in one of the few trees. The heat was suffocating. He wondered if, like before, he would get used to it or if he was growing too old, too accustomed to life back home. A lone bird, so high he could barely see it, a buzzard or crane, traced a taut wire between horizons. There were more clouds in the sky than usual, owing to the season. The bird passed behind one and came out the other side. It hadn't rained in more than a year. People feared the rain would fail to come again, so they did not speak of it except in whispers.

Insh'Allah.

⁂

The lorry growled into Marsabit long after dark. The trading center sat on a mountain with the same name, about a hundred miles south of the national border. The driver would spend the night and drive on the next day. From here he would take a different route, another lorry.

He disliked Marsabit. It was an ugly clearing of red clay carved out of the forest with pickax and hoe: The streets were rutted and everywhere littered with broken bits of glass and metal and the tattered black plastic of cheap shopping bags. It had a strange assortment of citizens. Young men and women from aid organizations riding around in bright new Land Cruisers, the cost of any one of which might have financed the town for a year. Livestock traders in dusty blazers and rubber boots. Women wrapped in red and blue scarves selling bundles of green leaves wrapped in newspaper. People chewed khat, or *miraa*, which was what they called it, as a stimulant when they talked late into the night. There were underfed children and beer-bellied bank clerks and wandering, barefoot mumblers, and young men in T-shirts and cotton trousers with nothing to do but listen to music outside the cassette store. There were priests, who did not walk but drove to their errands, then retreated behind the sanctuary walls, for the people outside badgered them no end for help.

He got a room: more concrete and rebar and warm blankets for nights cold from the elevation. Windows overlooked a central court where guests might park a vehicle, if they had one, and where workers hung laundry to dry and talked loudly and late into the night. He showered off the dust of the journey, which clung to his skin like a fungus. He ate at a café, ordering sour *injera* and chili-pepper stew—food difficult to get in the south and hard to avoid in northern canteens.

An old friend ran a shop at the crossroads. Tumal had not known he was coming. They smiled at each other in the dim yellow light of a single bulb. They talked of people they knew, caught up on Tumal's children—two had been born since he left, two others were now in school. Tumal asked his friend if he would sponsor one of his children in school. Just like that. He said he'd think about it. He did not tell the man about his wife.

He returned to his room, showered again, and lay awake in the dark. The town was haunted. There was this town and the town he remembered, the town from before, the town with her. They were the same and not the same. They were mirror images in a stereoscope.

The next morning he bought supplies: five kilos of tobacco, five kilos of sugar, several cartons of bulk tea leaves, three kilos of whole coffee berries, bags of hard candies—all gifts. For his own use: onions, garlic, rice, pasta, potatoes, plastic jerry cans for water, rope, cloth sheets, aluminum pots, spoons, cups, a couple of plates. He had his goods tied up in boxes and old gunnysacks and carried to the line of shops where lorries bound for the Chalbi lowlands waited before heading down the mountain to the desert. He got on the first one out, which left early that evening, just as the sun was turning red and the chill night wind was beginning to blow. The driver took on more than twenty people who rode atop the load of relief maize and crates of sodas. He stopped the lorry twice: first, before dusk, just outside town, to collect payments and get rid of freeloaders, and second, hours after dark, to let people stretch and pee.

He lay out on the firm sacks of maize. The smell reminded him of his grandfather's farm. He felt his body pitch and sway with the lorry as it bolted along the rutted track. He watched the stars against the black sky, obscured here and there by clouds. The air grew cold with the dark, and he wrapped himself in a cotton sheet he'd bought in Marsabit. He remembered that the first time they had come to this place they had ridden atop a lorry on such a night and she'd been bitterly cold. She suffered that night. He'd regretted asking her to come.

He gave her his own sheet to add to hers and that had helped. Eventually she'd forgiven him and wrapped the two sheets around both of their shoulders.

The lorry blew into Maikona around midnight with a great cloud of self-generated dust. The town was where it was because there was water. Nomads had been bringing animals to the Maikona wells for as long as they'd had animals, which was at least a couple thousand years. Traders had set up shops because it was a good place to meet herders. Then the colonial government, then the independent government, then the missionaries and NGOs. During droughts, the latter handed out relief maize and beans; offered medicine, even livestock; and collected impoverished herders in a sprawling shantytown made of dome-palm thatching and wattle. The people had asked for none of it, not at the beginning anyway, but they were hospitable—they'd take free food and whatever else.

He climbed down from the top of the lorry to a crowd of waiting young men, the highlight of whose day or night was meeting lorries. The occasional lorry was real excitement in a town where not much happened. It was like meeting the train, even if you didn't know anybody on it. Young men like these had been here last time. They were still here. Their names and faces were different. If they knew the driver, he might let them sit behind the wheel. They argued with each other for the privilege.

Someone remembered him, called his name, and others came to see and greet the *ferenji*. They all smiled. But they had nothing beyond good wishes for one another. He could not remember their names and could not ask about particular members of their families. They'd been schoolboys before. They knew him more by sight than acquaintance. He separated himself and went to sleep on a mat in front of a house owned by Tumal's brother.

In the morning he would set about finding his way back to Abudo's camp.

XIX

The present

Ado was in Elema's wife's tent, where she cooked what little she cooked while she was in mourning. Elema was off again in search of an automatic weapon. His wife and children had walked to a neighboring camp to visit relatives. He entered and found Ado weaving a mat for her daughter's wedding tent. The daughter was eleven or twelve and would marry in a few years. He sat on a stool to the left of the door, near the water containers. It was afternoon, the hottest part of the day, and the darkness of the tent fell over him like a cool shadow. She sat on a stool, close to the fire, to the right as he came in.

They sat opposite. He had the world to say, and she, from another, no way to hear it.

The tent, like all the others, was a dome, with a circular floor plan divided by a curtain between front, where the fire was, and rear, where the beds were. The armature was made of a hundred arched poles, themselves made from saplings that had been curved, cured, and treated with oil; each looked like a stout antique fishing pole in play. Through these were woven a lattice of smaller poles. Over the structure, women, who made and owned the tents, placed mats, which they had woven with sisal fibers. The mats were finished like the underside of a carpet on one side and left shaggy on the other, and the shaggy side faced outward as a sort of thatching. The tent looked like a coconut half buried in sand. A woman fastened her tools and containers to the armature inside, such as calabashes and tightly woven baskets for storing milk and wooden jars for oil and meat. The tent smelled of smoke and grease and butter and old rope.

Ado glanced up from her weaving as he entered. She lifted her eyebrows, an upswinging nod. She put down her project.

He said, *Ijole urgoftu?* Do the children smell good?

She shook her head as if he was silly. Her hand rose shyly to her face. She did not bother to answer.

She turned to the hearth.

He did not know what she expected.

He did not know what he expected.

Years ago, he had arrived from another planet. He met her husband at the wells. They became friends, gave each other things. He spent weeks in their company, disappeared for weeks on end, and then, usually without warning, turned up again. Children enjoyed him. He gave them sweets. He was funny, a tame baboon. Sun-whitened hair covered his arms and legs, and they liked to pet it. The old men enjoyed him. He gave tobacco, he asked questions, he listened. Then, after a couple of years, he disappeared, said good-bye, returned to his planet. They'd not heard from him for ten years—years of rain when malaria killed their children and animals died from cold, years of no rain when the dryness shriveled their breasts and children went to sleep with the same empty bellies that they'd risen to. Her husband died following an illness during which he could not walk but had to be carried on camels, when he did nothing but lie in bed. They took him finally to the government hospital at Marsabit, and that was where he died; the people there said they could do nothing. His family was not able to bury him, to bathe his body and lay it in a grave dug the day of his death, to put stones on it against the hyenas and the erosions of memory. And then, months later, the *ferenji*, Abudo's friend, the man who liked children and asked if they smelled good, who watched her as if he wanted something but did nothing, returned from his planet, showed up with no warning, and lay on a skin outside her tent as he had done before and drank milk and said almost nothing. He waited. Just waited.

He thought that must be what it was like for her. But he could only guess. Was he a burden? Was he amusing? Attractive? Did she want him there? Did she want him to sponsor her daughter in school? Did she wish she could talk with him, tell him her story? Should he speak of Abudo?

He'd no idea. None. He didn't remember the condolences one said, and anyway they would not be appropriate. He didn't know how—or even if—Dasse expressed remorse, other than in obvious ways, like a woman's shaving her head, or a son's or brother's letting his hair grow wild until the family sacrificed a camel. He'd never really paid attention to the ordinary discourses among people after death. They looked sad in the way people look sad. His studies had concentrated on outward signs and formal symbols, prayers and songs and events. The fact that a father's livestock was distributed to his sons, that the eldest got everything except what the father had specifically given to others. The brothers, who remained together until their father's death, usually split up afterward. That was what was remarkable about Abudo. Abudo shared with his younger brother. After their father's death, he and Elema remained together.

Ethnographic knowledge did him little good when he wanted something to say. He knew it was wrong to say the name of a person who had died, not because it would disturb the dead but because it would disturb the living. It was rude. But what could he say? He realized that, despite the time he'd spent with them, despite the knowledge he had described in field journals and scores of spiral notebooks, knowledge that had filled books and journal articles, despite all that *knowing*, he actually knew very little. He did not know what it was like to be them. He knew what it was like to be *with* them. But even adversaries knew what it was like to be in the same country, on the same field, in the same room. That did not mean they understood each other. He was sad about Abudo's death. One was sad when a friend died. But what sort of friends had they been? They had spent time together, and during that time they had enjoyed each other's company. He, at least, had enjoyed Abudo's company. After he left they did not communicate, not even once, not even through others. Their relationship had grown, held their attention for a while, and ended, the way a show came to a city, filled a theater, and moved on to the next town, leaving traces, old programs and ticket stubs, a fragment of melody.

He felt he should say something. But why? Surely Ado felt no reciprocal obligation to him. Had she known of his wife's death, she might have remarked on it, told the news to others, remembered her, thought of him. But she'd have done nothing. It wasn't a matter that required response. If you were present, that was another story: You helped dig the grave, you comforted the living, and then, within days, you moved on. The whole camp moved. Abudo had died months ago. Time passed. He showed up. Abudo's death was not on their minds, not as it was on his, like a headache. The ache was what brought him, the idea of getting rid of it. He and Ado knew each other through Abudo, and Abudo was not there, not anywhere. Except, he was still in their heads. Wasn't that why they were together in the tent just then, and wasn't that why she smiled when he entered—to say, *You are here*? He discovered that he didn't really know or understand any of it. He was walking at night without compass or flashlight. With nothing more than a book of matches lit in turns, casting pale glows of light briefly here and there.

She turned to the hearth, a pile of soft, white, cold-looking ashes. She did not dwell on his face. She stoked the fire with kindling from a pile of dead branches she kept nearby. She broke the branches into smaller pieces on her knee. As the branches began to smoke but were not yet ignited by the coals beneath the ashes, she reached for a blackened aluminum pot to her left and sloshed some water into it, rubbed it around, and poured it out on the ground. She was from force of habit frugal with water. She poured several cups of water into the pot and set it over the fire, which had come to life. The firelight flickered against the wall of the tent. He liked the warmth and closeness inside the tent, despite the heat outside, the feeling that the outside was off and away, like snow on a winter's night.

It was odd, the way he felt moved to tell her things. It was not that he thought she needed to hear them. He knew she didn't need or even want to hear them, that she took it for granted that he was sad. Words erased feelings; they ruined moments with the obvious.

He said what he said for himself.

He began in her language.

I remember him, he said.

Who? she asked.

You know. Whose name I do not say.

Eh.

She looked doubtful.

He was my friend, he continued. He gave me things. He gave me a man's staff, an *ororo*, so I would walk as a man. He killed goats and we ate together. He helped me buy a camel for loading so I could travel. He carved a bell for my camel.

Eh, she added after each statement.

I gave him things. I bought a sport coat for him in the capital.

He used the words *made cloth* because he could not think how to say *sport coat*. He was grasping for words.

I gave him a knife.

When your son was sick, I gave money for medicine, money for the doctor.

She turned her attention to the tea in the pot.

Had he said too much?

He switched to his own language.

What I want to say, the thing I liked, was he seemed to want to be my friend. Not many were like that. He was one.

It was better. His voice was relaxed, less anxious about making mistakes. He would not have known how to say *seem to want* in her language. He could have said that Abudo wanted his friendship, but it would have meant the same as if he'd said Abudo wanted food to eat. That would not have been right; that was not what he wanted to say.

He went on: He never seemed to expect more than he gave. He gave things before I asked, before I ever gave him anything. He was the only one. The rest saw me like they saw the priests, someone who gave, not someone with whom they could have a friendship.

He was different. He just gave.

She watched, curious about the language change. She did not stop him or complain that she did not understand. She poured milk into the brewing tea, stirred it, then leaned forward, elbows on her thighs, and listened or waited—he wasn't sure which, didn't care. She did not speak his language but knew what he was talking about and could hear his feelings, or so he imagined.

He taught me the names of things.

The first time I visited, we lay there in the back, on those beds, and he pointed out the containers on the wall and told me their names, and I repeated, and he corrected me.

Later he took me to *fora*, to his satellite camp, and we walked together and drank milk and blood and ate meat and he sang at night with the others and he taught me the songs.

I remember once, when the *olla* was shifting, he asked me to carry his spear to a woman, told me to give it to her. I did not know she was your mother. And she took the spear and admired it. And when she asked, I told her it was his. She gasped and dropped it. I wondered what I had done. I looked over at him and he laughed.

She answered his smile.

When I was about to leave I told him I'd run out of money, that my grant was over. You know what he said? He said I should ask and people would help if I wanted; they would give me what I needed. I didn't believe it. But the thought of staying intrigued me. I didn't know how serious he was, and anyway, I did not stay.

When I went home I wrote about what I learned, and that was what I did, and I continued to teach, and I did not come back.

Then I got a letter from the mission. They said he'd died, that he'd grown fat—*yagabat*, you say—and it was like all of you had died, like the world no longer had any of you in it. I'd written about an extinct people. I might as well have described an ancient Roman society. I didn't want to write or talk about any of you. I didn't want to utter your names.

She stirred.

Was she bored? Did she hear a change in his voice?

Eggi lam', he said. *Diko chala jedu feda.* Wait a minute. I've only a little more to say.

You knew my wife. He knew her, too. And she died, like him, for the same reason, and I don't know how either of them came by their illness, whether she gave it to him or he to her or they came by it independently.

I don't know that anybody could know now. The witnesses are dead. Only they know. Hell, I don't know if they know. They're not speaking to us. What killed them is around. It may kill you. I don't know. It might have killed me.

That's why I came back. I can't help. I don't know what I'm doing, and anyway, it's too late. Even if you have it, or Elema and others in camp, you'll never get rid of it. It's just here. There's nothing to be done. Forgive me. There's nothing.

⁂

She looked up when he finished. Then she took a cup and dipped it into the milky tea and lifted it in the air and poured a stream of it back to mix it, to cool it, to keep it from boiling. She lifted the pot off the fire and let it stand for a minute, and then with a cup ladled the tea through a strainer into another, larger cup, and handed it to him, and he held it and felt its warmth on his hands and blew across its surface, tea leaves floating there, chocolate brown, and sipped.

Chai dansa, he said. *Anan qufa*. The tea is good. Be filled with milk.

She smiled.

She picked up and continued her weaving and told him things, in her language, that he could barely make out. She told him about her sister, who was married and living in North Horr. She told him about her brother, whom he knew, a soldier down country, in Kakamega. He sent her things. Cloth. She showed him. She told him about her sick mother in Badda Hurri. She told him about her son, and he tried harder to follow. Godana was his name, though she did not say it. He had been with others in a *fora* satellite camp, west of Dukana. He was too young for *fora*. Something sudden, a surprise. Nighttime. He caught words. She made a spearing motion with her hand. There had been *shangila*, enemies, and they'd had guns—she used the down-country term, *bunduki*.

He watched her face. Her face was calm. She might have been telling him the price of goats.

Listening to her stories was hard, like reading words on a weathered gravestone.

He was glad she spoke. He had told her his news. She had told him hers.

When he emptied the tea cup he shook out the sodden leaves on the ground and handed the cup back to her. He pulled out his tobacco pouch and put a small chunk of tobacco in his mouth, between his cheek and gum. There was no thank-you. He didn't think there was a word for thank-you. If someone gave you a big thing, like an animal, you could say something like *many returns*. But gratitude, like grief or remorse, was assumed, and unspoken. That had always seemed rude to him. He found ways in lieu of thanks to be polite without being rude. He said, *anan qufa*, be filled with milk, which was odd but intelligible, the sort of thing an eccentric old man would say.

He wished her to be satisfied with milk, parted the curtained doorway, and stepped into the white heat of the afternoon.

ORDINARY SACRIFICES ARE *performed on particular days in the first half of the month, during the waxing moon. Marriages and* sorio hamtu, *however, happen on the third or fifth days of the waning moon, depending on the day of the week, Mondays and Thursdays being the best days. Thus Dasse link marriage, a ceremony especially associated with life, anticipating as it does the birth of children, and* sorio hamtu, *a ceremony associated with death but also with rebirth, the new life of a dead man's surviving family.*

XX

He and Ali skirted the southern slopes of the Hurri Hills, backs to the sun, morning shadows stretched long and thin before them like tree trunks against the red earth. The familiar smells of camp, of smoke and dung and milk, gave way to fresher, desert flavors: shaved cedar and leather, dust after rain, cucumbers, rose petals. A soft wind blew them forward.

His spirits lifted with the journey: He had felt the same lift, the sense of purpose, at the airport, and again moving north from the capital to Abudo's camp. Now it returned. They had a destination and route. These put new swing in his step.

Ali was just the opposite: sullen, sad to leave his new friend. She was close to his own age, wife of an older man. Spouses typically had romantic relationships outside marriage, with lovers their own age. Most wives were twenty, even thirty years younger than their husbands. They didn't like their partners having friends. But it was normal and expected. Her husband had gone to Maikona to visit relatives and sell goats. So Ali wanted to stay, at least until the husband returned. If he'd been sick, he might have asked to delay their departure. Ali would not ask to stay for a woman friend, though he would have liked to stay.

It had come to him to leave as surely and suddenly as it had come to him back home, with the news of Abudo's death, to go. He could not say what he had accomplished; he had not known what he wanted to accomplish. They would not discuss the dead, and even if they would, he lacked the language and perhaps the will. What was there to say? Perhaps he had simply wanted to see what was left. Perhaps he'd wanted to draw himself closer to Abudo, and in doing so recover something of her, square her in his memory. She was still there, of course, but oddly askew, blocked from view, like a figure sitting around the corner of a room, visible in the scythe-edge of profile: a curve of foot, a knob of knee and shoulder, a glance of cheek, the faint breath of perfume. She remained that way, obscure. Did he set her there in the corner, or did she withdraw? He had not managed to bring her back into view. He had, however, discovered that she was still there. The knowledge comforted him. Abudo's being tangled up in all this even buoyed him. He discovered that he actually wanted to believe they'd had the affair, that she'd gotten the infection then, from him, or he from her. The thought of them together like that compensated, evened the balance. Perhaps she had betrayed him, lived recklessly, selfishly. It was curious how conflicted he was thinking about it, wounded and relieved at the same time. It was confusing. She had loved him. He had hurt her. She had punished him. She had hurt him. They were even. In his own selfishness he was almost glad. He was like a kid who hurts a friend or sibling, then tries to make it up by saying, here, don't tell, hit me, hard as you can, it's OK, just hit me. She'd hit him. And it was all in his head.

⁂

He walked in front along the narrow trail between the stones, Ali behind, holding the camel rope. They startled a brace of sand grouse from under a *deka* bush beside the trail. He heard the sudden whir of rushing wings. He did not see the birds at first but streaks of light and shadow passing before them. Only when the birds rose above the horizon and got far enough away to be seen from behind did they become distinguishable as two birds. They darted from the stones like fighter jets from an aircraft carrier, climbed into a robin-shell sky, banked in separate directions, then gathered together again, one a little ahead of the other.

He scanned the ground for the nest, but they'd left so fast it was impossible to see where they'd been amid the rubble.

He liked sand grouse. They looked like athletic doves: pretty, dun-colored, except in the sun when their feathers were iridescent amber, like waxwings back home. Fast and angular. Even hawkish. Wings bent like swifts' wings.

They were big breasted.

In fact, they nursed their young as mammals do.

Sand grouse nested on the desert, far from water, and flew miles to springs and wells, over and over throughout the day. He'd spent hours watching them do this. They landed beside the water, at the spring's muddy banks. There were dozens, sometimes hundreds of them, depending on season and time of day and size of spring. They'd waddle to the waterline, like cows to trough, newcomers waiting in formation behind. As they got to the edge each lifted her breast feathers, like a woman lifting the front of her dress to sit down, and pressed them into the shallow water. Water runs from a duck, but it collects in a grouse's down, beading up in the soft, spongy fibers. Then, with a boom of collective wings, the front row lifted off and dashed back to suckle their young with water from their bosoms.

He liked sand grouse not because they looked a certain way or because they flew a certain way but because he knew certain things about them; he understood aspects of their behavior, and that made them nearer to him, part of his world.

He thought of the word *relation*, from Latin *re-latus*, to carry back.

Ali noticed the grouse but said nothing.

The anthropologist turned and with his face gestured in their direction.

Ali nodded without interest.

They're like camels, he said, in Ali's language, literally that the grouse *looked* like camels.

It was not exactly what he wanted to say.

The comment amused the boy. He smiled, cocked his head.

Eh, he said doubtfully. The color?

He was reaching for what he meant.

They nurse their young with breasts.

Wa! Is it? They have milk?

Water, water from the spring. In their feathers. They give their young water.

Then they're not camels, Ali said.

He paused a beat.

They're women, fetching water for children. Camels give milk. Women give water.

Women give milk, too.

Yes, but then they are camels.

Ali did not say they looked like camels.

He said they *were* camels.

That was the turn of so many of his conversations.

They meandered along but eventually stepped over the edge of his competence. His language was not strong enough to talk metaphysics, to play consciously along the divide of literal and metaphoric speech. He could not without help explore the implications of Ali's classifications. Were camels the prototype of milk-givers? Or was Ali playing poetically with analogies, disagreeing with the one he made, making another? How could he ask the question? To do that, one had to step outside the language and look in, and he could barely do that in his own language, let alone one he stumbled in like new shoes. He didn't know how to ask Ali about the range of ways to say something: His question was always, How do you say this or that? Or, What does this or that mean? And that was how Ali and others took his questions. They repeated the words of the question. Or they said it another way. He wanted to ask, Are women really camels? But of course they weren't, and they both knew it. He could not ask that. He suspected Ali meant more than that they were simply like camels because they fed their young milk.

Was it poetry if it wasn't meant to be poetry?

Was it poetry if the meaning depended on misunderstanding?

⁂

They'd left Abudo's camp without fanfare. Nomads, living on land that compelled mobility and fragmentation, were accustomed to arrivals and departures. Arriving was desired, so they marked it elaborately. Leaving was hard but inevitable, and they made it easy. There were few words for good-bye. Sometimes people would turn from conversations and simply go, just like that, walk away. One just left. The only departures that warranted ceremony were death and marriage, and then it was not for the departed so much as the left behind, the survivors, adjusting to the new world they inhabited without whoever was gone. Perhaps that was what he'd been up to the entire journey, a ceremony of sorts, a ritual of adjustment to a new world. Or was it to redeem the memory of the old one? Was there a difference?

Since they would be climbing and the air in the mountains would be cool, they set off in the morning rather than the middle of night. They left as the camp's camels left for pasture. They would not come back. Elema stood at the thorny gate of his corral and watched them go.

No one waved. Elema's son scrambled barefoot from his mother's tent and stood by his father and watched, his face screwed up in a look that was both amused and puzzled. The gate faced east, which was customary, so the rising sun shone in their faces and, for Elema and his son, transformed the two others and the camels into silhouettes. They circled round the south side of camp to avoid the lava cliffs to the north.

Ado had gone early that morning with other women to collect sisal fibers for making tents. They'd headed into the mountains to the east, while he and Ali would follow the slopes west to a pass and then cut across diagonally toward Balessa.

Ado had asked him to pass through the settlement of Badda Hurri. Her mother was there. Ado had given him money from the sale of a few goats and sheep to give to her mother. Ado wasn't clear about what it was for, some sort of ceremony: She had said *sorio*, a sacrifice, though it was the wrong month. The settlement was more or less on his way, and he agreed, glad to do something for his friend.

Their good-bye that morning consisted of catching each other's eyes and holding them a beat longer than they might have.

Nagayan gal, she said. Return in peace.

For a moment he thought she meant to return here, to this place, to her. Then he thought she probably meant for them, him and Ali, to return to their own homes in peace.

Elema's wife helped load the camels and returned to her own tent. Ali's friend did not emerge.

Elema stopped at the corral gate. *Nagayat*, he said.

He and Ali set off, the camels laden with water from the *lagga*, into the rolling, storybook hills of Badda Hurri.

The hills looked like weathered pyramids bunched in a range that seemed at once forbidding and inviting. They did not appear to be difficult to climb, but they were odd and anomalous in the flat and expansive landscape. They were so often shrouded with mist and clouds that, in the midst of a desert, they seemed possessed by supernatural forces. The desert lay at an elevation of about fifteen hundred feet above sea level and rose gradually and then abruptly into the hills of Badda Hurri, which peaked at around five thousand feet. The name meant *misty forest*, though most of the forest was gone, probably burned over millennia by pastoralists who preferred pasture to forest. In some of the valleys there were still groves of ancient trees: black-barked, set far apart in the grass, like oaks in a cemetery. But the slopes were mostly covered with grass and shrubs. The hills were misty because, like Marsabit, their elevation forced the warm winds from the distant sea to rise and cool, creating clouds. The hills got little rain: the grass and trees drew their moisture from the clouds themselves. When it did rain, the water quickly seeped into the ground. There was pasture in the mountains, but no reliable drinking water, which was why they were no more populated than they were.

The continent itself was a flat expanse, a huge plateau that rose precipitously from ocean shores and then leveled off and reached far and far again with few interruptions: these being river crevasses, gaping tectonic yawns, and seepages, millions of years old, of now-crusted magma. The place was huge beyond imagining, large enough to contain half the rest of the world's land surfaces. Despite the population growth of the last century, the continent remained underpopulated. Great swaths of it, like this one, had so few people that a traveler could walk for days and think he was alone, though he was never alone.

I ASKED DASSE *about the significance of performing* sorio hamtu *on the third and fifth days of the waning moon. You prefer even numbers, I said, so why now an odd number of days? The question prompted them to stop what they were doing to consider it. They shifted it right away from a question about* sorio hamtu *to that of marriage, which is also held on the third or fifth day of the waning moon. So why marry on the third or fifth day of the waning moon? One pointed out that the number of days was not the only odd number associated with marriage, that the household hearth consists of three stones, and the hearth represents the marriage. Another noted that adding the number of* sesuma, *or hearth stones, with the number of days gives an even number, either six or eight. I gathered that they thought my question deserved an explanation, but it was not a troubling problem for them. They did not reach far to resolve it. None of them thought to say that in both death and marriage the family experiences a loss, and that the odd number may indicate the missing member.*

⁂

They spent the first hours that morning picking their way along a faint trail heading northwest, which eventually joined another, more obvious trail. This one ran roughly north-south between the mountains and the Maikona wells, far to the south, beyond the flat horizon. They turned north onto it and climbed into a pass between the rounded pyramids.

The morning sun had climbed and was growing warm. He was thankful that the climb would take them into cooler air. They would cross the mountains in two days, reaching the settlement on top that night, and come out the end of the second day on the flat expanse northwest of the hills. From there they would set out for Balessa, where they would get water at Lagga Balal. They would visit other camps he knew, though not as well as Abudo's, and proceed south to North Horr, where he would visit the priest, who'd known them both, before returning with the camels along the Chalbi rim to Maikona. He would be glad to see the priest.

The trail climbed rapidly. Ali, young and lithesome as an antelope, easily kept pace with the steady camels.

He, however, was soon out of breath. But he was glad to be moving again. The land was grassier than it had been on the journey north from Maikona, blushed green by the recent rainfall. They passed desert flowers: roses and lilies that waved in the wind. Here and there stood old black trees, big-boned as oaks, scraggly, deep crevasses in the bark, reminding him of the trees that menaced the travelers in *The Wizard of Oz* or marked the night path of Ichabod Crane: storybook trees on storybook mountains. They didn't seem real. They were ideas of trees, just as the mountains were someone's ideas of mountains. They were mountains drawn by children, rounded, archetypal. Perhaps that was it. These mountains were here with the first humans. There was a good chance that an ancestor of ancestors, back in the original breath of the place, saw the same mountains, the same slopes, surely not much less eroded than they were now. Perhaps these were the prototypes of all mountains for all of human experience, laid down in what a famous anthropologist once called *genetic memory*, misting into view anytime someone dreamt of mountains or drew them from imagination.

They stopped around noon beneath one of the old oaks, hobbled the camels, and let them graze. They made a fire and tea with some milk Elema's wife had given them and sat and looked back the way they'd come across the flat and bleak plains, seen now from above, running with streaks of trails and seasonal rivers southward toward the wells. In the distance, more than one hundred miles away, he could see Marsabit Mountain, a gray smudge on the horizon. As the water heated he chewed tobacco. Ali's tobacco sack—a square of plastic paper torn from a bag of candies—was empty, and he gave him a fistful and added some chunks of *megado* salt, which they both used with tobacco. This was the best time of a journey, when they'd walked enough to have gone somewhere, spanned a distance, then sat to rest in shade and feel the wind and ease of their relaxed legs.

Ali al, he told the boy. Out is out.

It was what Abudo had said at almost the same moment on a different journey, to one of Abudo's camel camps. They were resting in the shade and Abudo said it and he understood the words but wasn't sure what they meant: Out is out. Since then he thought he'd come to know the meaning.

Ali smiled and spit. He shook tea leaves into the steaming water, and then, as it came to a boil, poured the milk into it, nearly a quart, which checked its boil. He stirred the tea with one of the mugs to keep it from boiling again and poured in sugar. Ali used too much sugar, but he said nothing; the boy did not think the *ferenji* knew the first thing about making tea. Ali removed the fire-blackened pot from the stones around the flames and set it on the ground to cool a moment, then filled their mugs. He did not use a screen to catch the sodden tea leaves.

We should reach Badda Hurri today. The town. Tonight.

Eh, Ali agreed.

Should we camp there, or should we camp outside it?

He felt entitled to make the decision himself, but he included the boy. The truth was he was unsure, and he wanted the boy's opinion.

Ali set his tea on the ground beside him and studied the ground at his feet. He had a stick in his hand, and he twitched the soil with it, turned a loose blade of grass, flicked an insect away.

He said he did not know.

The town, he said, is bad. There are witches. There's Ayana.

Ayana was a cult of sorts—borne from the north, vaguely associated with Islam—that people who did not belong thought was evil but whose participants claimed had powers to heal sickness and correct misfortune. *Ayana* meant *spirit.* A sick person—it was usually a woman—might be possessed by a spirit that was making her ill. An Ayana specialist would help her and her family identify the spirit, speak to it, and not so much make it go away as make it happy, so it wouldn't keep making the person sick. There were rumors of nighttime bacchanals, the sort of things you heard about marginal groups everywhere on earth: that they danced licentiously and sacrificed children and drank their blood. Ayana followers avoided *ferenji* because they associated *ferenji* with missionaries, and missionaries preached against Ayana. So did many Muslims.

But it'll be cold, the boy added. We don't have blankets. We should sleep inside to stay warm.

Perhaps, he thought, they should have gone around the mountains.

He had not thought about Ayana. Elema had not reminded him. Ado had not mentioned it. When he was here before he had heard there was Ayana at Badda Hurri, but not such a presence as Ali's tone suggested.

A couple of crows peered down at them from the limbs of the

tree. He wondered irrationally whether they were innocent crows. He shook his head of the thought, as if trying to shake water from his ears. He threw a rock at the crows and they lifted and coasted in the steady wind to the nearest tree, twenty-five yards away, where they alighted, wrapped their wings about them like capes, and faced the humans again, eager for scraps. Why was he responding to nonsense fears? Ayana was a sect, a religion, no more dangerous than Protestants or Catholics. He'd met Ayana followers before. His assistant's father had been one of their leaders—a strange man, he thought, but harmless. The worst they did, he thought, was fleece goats from vulnerable women in exchange for pseudo diagnoses and cures. He had heard that and believed it. But doctors everywhere did that. He'd also heard, when he was here before, that Ayana had loyal followers, that their numbers were growing, that the cures actually worked.

Do you know anyone we could stay with? he asked. The fact Ado was sending money to her mother suggested that she was in no position to take them in.

My father does.

Have you ever been there?

No.

Is there a name, someone your father knows?

Eh. There's a man who is *halkum*, of my mother's family.

We'll find him. We'll be OK.

He was reassuring himself. He wasn't sure Ali needed reassuring.

Chufa sawasawa, he said. It's all OK. The two words mixed their language with the national language, a habit he'd got used to because he was undisciplined with languages but also because he'd heard young people do it and he liked the way the words sounded together.

They finished their tea, packed things up, pissed, fetched the camels, which had wandered away to browse while they rested, and, leaving only a smoldering fire and a soggy clump of loose tea leaves for the crows to pick at, set off into the mountains.

AT A SMALL olla *of six tents, more than a hundred people, including many from surrounding camps, gathered on the morning of the third day of the waning moon of Soom D'era for Wario Tandi's* sorio hamtu. *Wario had been well known, and a* d'abella, *a priest of sorts. Many came because they knew the family and because they knew that a camel would be slaughtered and everyone would get a share of meat and coveted hump fat, or* gobo. *I arrived at six o'clock, bleary-eyed from an all-night vigil at a wedding at a different camp. It was dawn, still cool from the night. The sun had yet to rise, but the eastern sky was laced with rose-colored clouds. A three-quarter moon hung heavily in the western darkness. Normally, things are just beginning to stir at this time of day. But at Olla Wario, women were already preparing great pots of tea and milk for the guests. Cow skins had been brought out of tents, and* d'abella, *who made up nearly a quarter of the crowd, were sitting or lying on skins, chewing tobacco, and visiting.*

⁂

They had told each other a story, the same story. It was their agreement, a myth of sorts, and it had satisfied: She made herself into a nurse, a caregiver, and her illness owed itself to that impulse, the help of another. Nothing about the circumstances of the woman in the forest had changed: He had no doubts, even now, that the event had occurred, and it was still quite possible that she had been infected then. That much was true. He knew that, or felt he did.

But the pictures in her journal—what had they meant? They were pictures, lines and smudges on the surface of paper. It was thick artist's paper that had heft to it, and that heft added weight to their content. They were, he told himself, only drawings. Fictions. But fictions are interpretations of sorts: They are not random; they are motivated by an interest, a matter of the heart. The pictures meant something. He just could not be sure what.

In the months after he'd seen them he had revisited the pictures, gone down the steps to the sunlit studio, not every day or every week but now and then, to confirm that they were there, not figments of his imagination.

Had she merely imagined them? Was that enough?

Did she feel this urge? Did it matter? Could an artist not imagine freely, without having to shoulder responsibility for the images and thoughts?

If she had done this, these acts with Abudo, and recorded them in her journal, was it really, in the end, so terrible? He and his wife had had the relationship that they had had, whether she had done these things or not. He could not think of another he'd have rather had. He had nursed her. They had lain together, forehead to forehead, and breathed each other's breaths, told each other the matters of their hearts. They had become, in her illness, something of an old couple together, a couple that didn't need to speak, eye contact being enough, and sometimes not even that: They'd known each other well. That was the intimacy that came from being there, enduring the journey. Her feelings for him were not, in themselves, affected by these acts, though he knew his for her had been. In ways he had not fully imagined.

The image of her with Abudo, the trouble it caused him, fixed in his mind, fixed her in his mind. She was there and living and large. If nothing else, it was a way to keep her, hold on to her as otherwise the memory of her would dim and fade away. She might have become ill separately. The two events—one a fact, the other, what? An imagining? An interpretation?—the two events might be unrelated. It was their two-ness, the coincidence of implication, an illness and a drawing of an act that might have induced the illness: That was a sort of evidence. It seemed weak to him if he thought about it, but it gave him conviction, made the scenario plausible. He even found himself attracted to the story. It made sense of things, and wasn't that what interpretations did: made sense of things?

A SCORE OF *younger men was busy cutting branches from surrounding* d'ad'acha *trees,* acacia tortilis, *and dragging the thorny branches near the village where they would be handy for constructing the* hos. *The* hos *is a substantial dome structure, sometimes two or three times the size of a tent, made entirely of thorn branches. It is built for* sorio hamtu, *and in its shade* d'abella *will eat their share of the meat. It will never be used again but left to collapse on its own in the weather over the coming months or years.*

◆

The sky cleared for a while early in the afternoon but clouded over as the day waned and as they rose in elevation. They were soon enveloped in windswept fog. If not for the deep rut of a trail amid the grass before them, they'd have been hopelessly lost. They stuck to the trail. Figures emerged in the fog, as if they, too, were carried by the wind—a dark tree, a bush—and blew away behind them as they passed. Once they met a man walking the other way. He wore a dark western suit and tire sandals and a floppy hat that he held on his head with one hand against the wind. He did not look at them and mumbled something only after they greeted.

Wara buyo, Ali said.

He had always heard that there were more Borana in Badda Hurri than Ali's people. Borana, a highland cattle-keeping group, were more numerous than their neighbors and more aggressive. While Dasse lived in matted—or *dasse*—tents, Borana were people of grass houses, *wara buyo*. Some believed that hundreds of years ago Ali's ancestors fell under Borana influence, that that was why they now spoke the same language and why they currently lived in uneasy symbiosis with one another, Ali's people the clients of the more powerful Borana.

He'd also heard that Ayana was popular among Borana.

They passed a lonely sod structure, a farm, dimly visible through the fog from the path. The place looked abandoned, but someone was surely inside. They kept on. Soon they passed another, and several women passed on the trail, going the other way, and did not speak, even when greeted.

You should ask at one of these houses for the friend of your father, he said.

Ali gave him the camel rope. He stood with the puzzled camels, and Ali ran up to a house and shouted. He could see a door crack.

Ali spoke with the person for a while, and then the person, a woman, emerged and stood and gave Ali directions, gesturing into the fog.

Ali returned, and he asked what he'd learned. Ali gave a noncommittal grunt and gestured with his nose. They kept on the path, nothing but grass to either side. They soon came to a fork, and Ali took the left prong, and when the path met a dirt road, they turned right on it. The road was carved deeply into the reddish clay soil, tufted with grass at the top of the banks on either side. The gloom made it difficult to see much beyond the edge of the road.

In ten more minutes they came upon the settlement. He'd been through here before. But then, it had been on a lorry bound farther north. He'd seen farms back home with more buildings. They were structures encased entirely by corrugated iron sheets, some of which had come loose and banged in the wind. Few people were out on the street. No children. One fellow had whitish pants and a black sport coat and a walking staff. He was walking away from them. A pair of dogs nosed offal in the lee of a building. Doors were closed against the cold. There were no signs over the doors, no advertisements for what happened inside. He could see dim lantern light leaking from some of the cracks. He couldn't tell if these were businesses or houses; they looked more like businesses to him. But for what? There was a stockade. Perhaps there was livestock trading.

ANOTHER GROUP OF *perhaps twenty-five men had already left the* olla *in search of an entire* d'ad'acha *tree, to be erected immediately west of the camp and used as the central pole and roof of the* hos, *a ceremonial shelter. A* d'ad'acha *is an umbrella tree, with a tall branchless trunk rising to a sprawling horizontal ceiling of thorn-laden branches. The tree for the* hos *should be immaculate, having never been trimmed of branches for making livestock corrals. When the men had chopped the tree down, they lifted it into the air, after which point it would not and should not touch the ground until it was placed in a hole dug for it back at the* olla. *The men lifted the tree by its trunk and laid the trunk along their shoulders. Others helped to brace the tree with* hoko, *a special tool for manipulating thorny branches, like a shepherd's staff, with a crook at one end and a Y at the other. As they returned to the* olla, *they sang* nyar, *a chant of nonsense syllables, something like "*iyoiyoiyo...,*" which would not stop until the tree was in place. It is the same chant men use when carrying a sick or dying person over a long distance, and it is similar to* yamu, *a song for drawing water for animals at the wells, which has words for verses but has a background chorus of nonsense syllables, like "*iyamiyamiyam....*"

⁂

He followed Ali, walking beside him now that they were off the trail and on the wide muddy road. They stopped beside the third building on the right. Ali handed him the camel rope again and walked up on a porch of rough boards and whispered something inside. Nothing. He raised his voice. A man answered. Ali opened the door. He tied the rope around a porch strut and followed.

Inside was a large room with a dirt floor and a wall opposite with a doorway and a curtain drawn across it. The room was lit by a smoky kerosene lantern. An old wood-frame bed stood unevenly against the far wall. There was a cow skin on the bed in lieu of a mattress, with a frail old man sitting on it, one knee up by his chin, the other bent and tucked beneath him. He was wrapped in a tattered felt blanket. He was apparently blind, for he looked toward them but at neither of them, and his eyes were milky, as if they were full of snot. Ali and the man greeted, then he and the man greeted, and the old man cocked his head to new attention when he heard the unusual accent, but the man did not remark on it.

The old man asked Ali about himself, who his father was and his grandfather, and he could tell that from these answers the old man knew exactly who Ali was though he'd probably never met Ali. He knew the lineage and knew that his family married that one and in that way knew Ali. The old man did not ask about the other man.

The old man said that his granddaughter was out and could not make them tea and they hadn't any milk anyway. He and Ali insisted that they were satisfied without tea: *Yakuf, anan kufa*.

Ali explained to the old man that they were traveling from Abudo's camp at Toricha to Balessa, that the *ferenji* had worked here years ago and had come back to visit. He said that they wanted to stay the night and continue on the next morning. Ali mentioned that they had a gift for Ado's mother. He used simple language, for the old man's ears were bad and the wind made noise on the roof and Ali had to shout. The *ferenji* easily followed what Ali said. The old man did not respond, except to nod the same way he'd nodded to hear who they were, to acknowledge a fact. He did not have to welcome them to the house, for of course they would stay with him—one did not seek or need permission for such visitations with family, however distant. He asked instead for news about Abudo's camp. Ali had referred to it as Elema's camp. The old man knew Abudo was dead. He asked about Elema. He asked about the rains, whether there was grass. He asked about Ali's father in Maikona, whether there was relief maize and if Ali knew when the government lorry would bring maize to Badda Hurri. He still did not ask about the *ferenji*, who was tired from the trip and content to sit and listen and watch the lantern flame.

Soon the granddaughter returned, banging on the door for the old man to open it, then surprised to find it ajar, to find others inside. She entered timidly, like a cat, and without introductions stepped across the room through the curtain to the back room, which he decided must be the kitchen and where she slept. The logic of these permanent houses was different from the tents, where the hearth was in front. A light flicked across the curtain, the pan of an electric torch, then a lantern squeaked and glowed. Against the blow of wind on the corrugations, he heard the girl cracking sticks for a fire, which soon added a warmer glow to the curtain and shimmered there like evening sun on a river. He could smell the welcome smell of wood smoke and hear the cold wind outside, the occasional spit of rain against metal, the drone of Ali telling the old man news and the old man's hummed responses. The old man fumbled shakingly with a piece of cloth the size of a napkin and opened it to a wad of tobacco, some of which he put in his mouth. He followed suit, brought out his tobacco, chewed, and spit on the earthen floor, using his foot to cover the saucy spittle with dirt. He made a note to himself to give the old man a few fistfuls of tobacco when they unloaded the camels. Soon the granddaughter emerged with a cup of tea in each hand and gave these to the two guests, not meeting their eyes. It was strong tea with sugar, no milk. She said something to the old man, and he told them again that there was no milk, and both of them said the polite thing, which was *anan kufa, anan kufa*, be satisfied with milk, a blessing.

THE TREE'S ARRIVAL *initiated a flurry of organized chaos. While several men held the tree erect in a large posthole dug for this purpose, others filled the hole with earth and stones and tamped it down. The rest, swept up in the moment, ran back and forth bringing great fans of thorn-studded branches and set them in the outer holes. The thorns in the upper reaches of the outer branches entangled with the thorns in the lower reaches of the tree's branches, forming a seamless canopy, like a bristly weeping willow, all around the tree from top to ground. Men darted among one another, all at a trot, with unwieldy branches, and tossed them at the growing structure, where they clung in the thorns. Two men, demonstrating considerable bravado, climbed the outer walls to the top, protected by nothing but the soles of their sandals, their bare legs nicked here and there by thorns, and pressed loose branches into the roof with their* hoko. *A small door, mirroring that of the Dasse tent, was left open on the eastern side of the* hos, *facing the encampment.*

⁂

They unloaded the camels and set their gear inside. There was a corral behind, a large pen really, where the old man once kept his own cows, and where they now put the camels.

Ali got directions to Ado's mother's house from the granddaughter. It was not far. Nothing was far. The town was little more than a collection of outhouses. The granddaughter told them the house they sought had a red door, and they found it easily.

He called from outside. Nothing. He called again. The door scraped open. It was a young man, Ali's age. Ali explained why they had come. The boy let them into a room not unlike the old man's, and in the corner on a bed lay Ado's mother, blank-eyed in the lamplight, showing no sign of greeting or fear. He had known her years before but hardly recognized her now.

She was a ghost of Ado. He could still see the resemblance. She looked like his wife, he thought, but that was the sickness.

He gave the boy the money. The boy smiled. He said the money would buy two *reeti*, female goats.

He marveled that they'd anticipated the money, knew it was coming, knew how much, knew what it was for. Ado must have sent word ahead. She had not said her mother was as sick as she was. He acknowledged the woman with the customary evening greetings, but she did not answer, gave nothing in return. He resisted the urge to go to the bed, to straighten her blankets, to arrange her body.

The boy shook his head. He said her condition was *hamtu*, very bad, but that now—he waved his hand with the money—she would get better.

He said nothing.

THE HOS IS *a symbolic obversion of the tent. It shares the tent's dome shape. But where the tent is shingled with soft mats, the* hos *is shingled with thorns; where the tent faces west, away from the wind, the* hos *faces east, into the wind; where the tent sits on the eastern side of the village, the* hos *sits on the western side; and where the tent is owned and built exclusively by women, the* hos *is built exclusively by men. If one were to make a* mona, *a corral for animals, into a house for people using the same materials, he would construct a* hos. *Men build a similar structure, called* waab, *for camel calves, to give them shade from the sun and protection at night from hyenas and lions.*

XXI

The door rattled. The granddaughter had locked it after they returned. Someone outside banged. Banged again.

The old man shouted, *Eh!*

The others heard only a grunt in response, or growl.

The old man called his granddaughter, who came through the curtain and walked to the door and looked doubtfully over her shoulder at the old man.

He wondered whether she was afraid. She unbolted the door, stepped back, and retreated to the back room. The door swung open with a clatter, aided perhaps by the wind. A huge man wrapped in a felt blanket entered without greeting and stood for a moment and looked at them and closed the door behind him with one arm. He wore a beard and a white turban, and the irises of his eyes, instead of being dark like the others, were white or blue; he could not tell which in the poor light. Not snotty like the old man's but clear. The big man's eyes seemed to glow.

You have guests, he told the old man but looked at the *ferenji*.

Guests, he continued without the old man's answer, who are you?

There was no greeting. It was abrupt and rude. Even he felt this, though his own people did it all the time, the question for them being a sort of greeting, at least if it was asked with a smile and an outstretched hand. The man did not smile. The question, delivered without the polite preliminary of remarks about mutual strength and peace and the state of the rains or drought, felt like a mugging. Ali said nothing. He deferred to his elders. The *ferenji* took a moment to respond. That was fine. The big man could wait.

He said his name.

Where are you from? the big man asked.

America.

What do you want?

He was unsure how to answer. He didn't know how to explain what he was doing. Ali had told the boy at Ado's mother's house that the white man was traveling to Balessa.

We're going to Balessa, he said. We're visiting friends in Badda Hurri on the way.

Who are your friends? This man?

He thought to turn the conversation.

Maqa kanke enu? he asked the big man. Literally, who is your name?

Duba, the man said.

Duba *ka enu?*

Duba Kalacha. *Ani chifa* Badda Hurri.

Eh, the chief, he echoed.

He thought it probably wasn't true, but he didn't know who the man was and didn't know whether it was wise to challenge him. Boru Dulacha was chief of Badda Hurri. He knew that much. But Boru spent most of his time north of the mountain, on the border, at a place called Forole, which was included in the division. Duba could be Boru's deputy. It was customary for deputies, when the chief was away, to call themselves chiefs. If he were the chief, he'd have been to school and would have used the national language to speak with the *ferenji*.

Karatasi me? the big man asked, holding out his hand. Where are your papers? He used the national language for the word *papers*, and he said papers rather than passport or visa because his own language had no words for such.

They're in our gear, over there, he answered.

Bring them, the man said, and sat himself on a stool and waited as well for the girl to bring him a cup of tea.

The old man said nothing, only listened, lips puckering occasionally to spit, hands kneading the shabby cloth of his tobacco sack.

He and Ali stood. Ali held the torch while he rummaged through his satchel, found the passport, and stepped over to the big man, now sipping tea and talking to the old man, who did not appear to be listening.

Ho, he said, holding the passport out to the man.

Chufa? Everything?

Eh.

The man opened the passport and inspected each page carefully, nodding his head as though he were finding things in order, turning pages after pauses.

He realized then that the passport did not matter so much. The big man was reading in a way that suggested he wasn't reading—or didn't know how—pausing as long over blank pages as stamped ones, including the page with the current visa, a simple six-month tourist visa, without bothering to study them. He knew only that chiefs looked at travelers' papers.

He took his time. He turned every page. Then he closed the book.

Why have you come here if you're going to Balessa? he asked.

He thought that was what he asked. The man spoke quickly with a clenched jaw and was hard to understand. He heard the word *arma*, here, and he heard *Balessa*, and he guessed the man wanted to know why they had come here on the way to Balessa. Anxious, tired, flustered by the intrusion, he didn't know how to say what he needed to say.

He hesitated, looked at Ali. Ali spoke.

He is going to Balessa from Toricha, not from Maikona. He is traveling with camels, on foot. It is a long way. Going over the mountains is shorter than going around. It is also not so hot. The *ferenji* wanted to walk across the mountains with camels. He wanted to see the scenery. That is why we are here.

Ali did not mention the money for Ado's mother.

He could not tell from looking at Ali whether the boy felt fear or respect for the big man, and he thought that the same word—*sodaa*—covered both. He wondered whether there was really a difference between them. Maybe it had to do with the flow of power, whether power was given or taken—but when, he wondered, is it ever just one or the other?

Ali spoke. The big man glared at him.

Stay. In the morning I'll return.

He turned to go, the passport in his fingers.

The *ferenji* asked for his papers back.

The big man hesitated.

He didn't wait. He stepped forward and took his papers. He held the man's eyes. The eyes were blue as lawn flowers, with large black pupils that seemed to grow larger. The man opened his eyes wide and breathed deeply through his nose, then let the air out through his mouth. Duba would have been handsome, except for the strange eyes and his size, easily a foot taller and thicker than other Dasse, though not taller than he.

Chifa Boru *argu feda*, he said. I want to see Chief Boru.

He thought the big man was bluffing about being chief. He thought the mention of Boru's name, the fact he knew it, would add strength to his claim on the passport.

Tomorrow, the big man said. Now you stay here.

But for tone and context it might have been an invitation.

The big man opened and shut the door, and they heard the crunch of his heavy sandals on the road as he walked away.

He sighed, turned to Ali and then to the old man, who had sat quietly throughout. Ali put some tobacco in his mouth.

Who is the big one? Ali asked. He said *nama gudha*, big man, which could mean literally big or could mean impressive, important, or both.

The old man, who'd shown no particular interest in the exchange but stared blankly into the room, turned toward their voices and rolled his blind eyes.

He laughed. He couldn't help himself. Ali joined him.

The old man said: You asked for Boru. Boru will not come. He is away. This one is strong.

What will he do? he asked.

Imbeku, the old man said. I don't know.

WHEN THE HOS, *the thorn shelter for the old men, was finished, Wario's sons went with others to the camel corral to fetch a male camel, one that had not been used for stud or loading but kept only for meat, and led it back to the* hos. *The camel, having never been trained, balked and bucked and roared the entire way, crazed by the strange ropes and crowds. This was a dangerous operation, for camel legs are long and strong. It seemed miraculous to me that no one was hurt. It took some time and the concerted effort of nearly twenty men. The painfully futile struggle of the camel brought back a certain solemnity to the participants that had been lost in the excitement of building the* hos. *The arrival of the camel prompted women, standing near their tents, to weep. Wario's eldest son, wrestling with the reluctant beast, shouted at the women to stop. What are you crying for? he said. This is not your father. This will please your father.*

❖

He and Ali made a bed out of the cow skins on the floor in the room with the old man. They piled their things nearby. The girl brought a large tin plate, a serving platter, of cooked beans and maize, chewy, filling, from which they all ate together. He had lost his appetite but ate anyway, knowing he'd need strength tomorrow. He thought maybe they should leave in the night, before the big man came back, but that would be impossible. There was no way to keep it secret. He would come, and then it would be worse. Besides, they didn't know the way.

He went outside to get some fresh air. The house was filled with smoke. He'd grown accustomed to sleeping outside. He wondered how he would sleep with the smoke, and he wondered how he would sleep with the thought of Duba on his mind. He chewed his tobacco, and after he spit that out he brushed his teeth. The camels ignored him. Perhaps they were sleeping. One of them resumed chewing, but he supposed they chewed even in their sleep.

Inside the oil lamp glowed dimly. The old man lay on his bed and appeared to sleep. His granddaughter sat beside him on the bed. She glanced up as he entered and looked away. Ali was already wrapped in his sheet. The room was smoky, but he thought perhaps less so now that the girl had stopped cooking. Wind was blowing through the cracks and would eventually freshen the room. He lay down and pulled the sheet over his head from habit of sleeping outside with the wind but also against the light.

WHEN THE CAMEL *was in place, facing east, just to the north of the door to the* hos, *the sons of Wario Tandi began an elaborate ritual of blessing, or anointing, the camel. One of the younger sons brought a* gorfa, *a milking bowl, full of camel's milk, and handed it to the eldest, who stood south of the camel, on the camel's right side. The eldest son drank some of the milk, made the camel drink some of the milk by dipping its muzzle into the bowl, then poured the milk over the camel from head to tail, and finally splashed some milk with his hand on its underbelly. He handed the bowl to the next son, who did the same, and then the third. Then, using their hands or sticks instead of milk, the grandsons blessed the camel, in order of birth, followed by Wario's brother, and lastly the other men, according to clan seniority. The men should be barefoot; they either removed their sandals or at least pulled their heels out of the back strap while they blessed the camel. Several of the grandsons were infants or toddlers. They were frightened and screamed their reluctance to go near. Fathers picked them up and rubbed their bodies against the camel's neck and hump, laughing self-consciously at their sons' fears. They set them down at a safe distance, or put them into their mother's arms.* D'abella *did not participate but stood and watched. All the while, a group of men held the wide-eyed camel to keep it from bolting.*

He must have slept, for he awoke and found the old man's lamp was out. It was dark and cold. He could make out nothing inside the room. No stars. He was dizzy from the emptiness until he closed his eyes and saw the odd star patterns within his eyelids.

He slept some more. The sound of footsteps woke him.

The wind had stopped blowing. It was quiet except for the sound of people walking. He rose on his elbows to listen. People were passing outside. He rose to his feet and wrapped his sheet around his shoulders and went out to see. He saw people walking along the road. He could not see them clearly. The moon was obliterated by the clouds and mist. He sensed people more than saw them, heard the noise their feet made on the road, a sense of movement in the darkness, shadows within shadows. One figure came round the corner of a house with a flashlight that bounced as he walked and lit the calves of people in front. They were walking together, but no one was talking. He had not thought there were so many people in the town. They must have come from surrounding farms. He could not tell whether they were men or women or both. He thought the one with the flashlight was a man judging by his feet. He fell in behind, following the faint light of the beam twenty or thirty feet ahead. They went out of town the way he and Ali had come in. They left the town and then left the road, funneling into single file along a path into a sloping dell. Ahead he could see a fire: a strange thing to see at night, outside. People made fires for cooking. Inside. They rarely made fires outside at night except for some sort of ritual purpose, like a wedding night or the birth of a son, when the grandmother made a fire to burn the child's umbilical cord. This fire reminded him of a wedding fire, though there were no tents around. He could see the profiles of people against the fire. Many had carried pieces of firewood and, as they approached, placed the firewood in a pile. They sat or stood in tight circles near the fire, not around it, focused on each other, not the flames. By the firelight he saw that the groups were mixed men and women, which was as strange as the fire: Women and men seldom gathered like this in groups. Even at weddings women sang in one place and men in another. There were thirty or forty people. They had not been talking while they walked, but now he could hear them mumbling to one another, like the noise of bees in a beehive, a low apian drone. He stayed back and thought foolishly that he could not be seen. But his white sheet, wrapped around him against the cold, glowed in the firelight no matter how far out he stood. The group sensed his presence. They stopped their murmuring and looked. A figure rose from one of the groups and walked over and took his hand and led him to the congregation. He sat with a clutch of participants very near the fire. He felt its warmth through the cloth against his skin. He was thankful for the warmth, chilled as he was by the air and his uncertainty.

WHILE THE CROWD *stood in a wide semicircle, the camel was put down on its knees, its resting position, and its bent legs were tied together so it could not stand. More than a dozen men braced the body from either side, and another man held its head, pulled it to the side, and exposed its neck. A camel's death is an impressive sight. The slaughter is faced by all with rapt attention and awe. Gallons of blood gush from the wound onto the ground with the force of an open fire hydrant. The animal seems to deflate; its long neck relaxes, its doe-eyes fade, its flanks quiver, and finally its head is laid to rest on the ground, like a sleeping giant. The men who had worked so hard to hold the camel down now took pains to keep it from rolling over on its side. Isakho, old man Wario's eldest son, poured the remaining milk from the* gorfa *into the flowing blood.*

⁂

Out of the darkness came the big man, Duba, striding across the grass, not along the path, not from town, coming from a new direction, from farther out in the darkness. He wore a *kikoi* around his waist, but he no longer had the blanket over his shoulders. He was naked from the navel up. He was powerfully muscled and big-waisted as a wrestler. His turban was gone, and his hair stuck out like Medusa's. His eyes glowed in the firelight, as blue as phlox, phosphorescent as stars. His eyes were his charisma and he used them, glancing at the different groups, as much for them to see him as for him to see and monitor them. He stepped to the fire. The group shifted and made room for Duba near the fire. His eyes ceased to glow with his back to the fire. All the anthropologist could see was the big man's silhouette against the light and the crazy head of fibrous tentacles that emanated from it.

He wished he had not come, that he had not been curious about the people walking in the night, that he had bypassed Badda Hurri altogether, that he had not returned, that he had stayed home, for there at least the demons were familiar. He felt that there was only harm and damage here, though he could not decide what sort of harm. He had come out of the house in the dark. He had walked with people to this pasture, just as years before he had walked on moonlit nights with youth from the settlements to their dances. He had come tonight not because he was a scholar intending to write but because he was curious what they were up to, because he wanted to see. As he had come he had been unafraid. His feet had led him and he had followed. Now that he was here with them, he was afraid because he could not leave. He was no longer walking, going somewhere. He was here.

It began like a wedding night, with singing, except now men and women were huddled together instead of in separate groups. All were sitting. The fire flicked yellow on their faces. They were not smiling.

Despite the specialness of the moment, the ritual feel of the event, or perhaps because of it, their faces seemed neutral, flat. They might have been waiting out the ride of a bus or sitting alone under a tree, but they were together in this great group at an odd time, the middle of the cold night with a fire.

Perhaps, he thought, they were entranced or prepared to be entranced.

Perhaps, he thought, he did not know how they experienced this moment.

When the singing began it was the big man who started. He shouted more than sang, words the anthropologist could not follow. He seldom heard the lyrics of songs, even in his own language. It was almost impossible for him to pick out words sung with a melody. The music distracted him. The pattern was the same as songs at a wedding: call and response, the leader shouting out short sentences, like lines in a poem, the rest answering with a singsong chorus about the same measure but quicker, more energetic. The lead passed to others. He knew from before that these songs told a story or built an image or developed a theme—of the achievements of heroic individuals, for instance, or the prowess of cooperating warriors. The lead passed from the big man to others, including women, and on to people in other groups.

Men and women began to stand and dance together, jumping in the air, springing on flexed knees and feet. They had a stiff cow skin on the ground, and they pounded the skin with their feet. Their feet against the skin made a loud, drumming sound. Two partners would dance, jumping together, pushing off each other in the air with their chests, like lekking grouse. Beside them, two others beat time on long straight sticks that they held together, parallel, and clacked in complicated rhythms. Not everyone danced. People took turns. Some remained sitting on rocks or cross-legged on the ground, their bodies marking the rhythm. The movement was more vertical than horizontal. They didn't sway. They rocked their heads up and down, kept time by raising and lowering their shoulders. The dancing went on for at least an hour. He had not joined the singing except to hum. He thought it would last all night, for wedding dances last all night, ending only with the rising morning star.

What he saw in the people was what the old anthropologists called *communitas*. It wasn't that people sang and moved. It was their singing and moving together, in unison, that embedded each in the collectivity. It reminded him of the concerted behavior of an orchestra or a hive of bees, humming into existence an emergent energy with which they could dance all night.

WHEN THE CAMEL *was dead, the eldest son ran to his father's tent, collected the old man's clothes, sandals, stool, wooden coffee bowl, hatchet, and the metal parts of his spear, and brought them back to the camel. He filled the* gorfa *with blood from the still-oozing wound and spattered the blood on his father's possessions, in this way cleansing them so that they might be used again by his family. The spear, the dead man's most important remnant, his symbol, was given afterward to his brother. Had he no surviving brother, his eldest grandson would have inherited the spear. Meanwhile, the sons daubed their own foreheads and those of their sons with blood from the camel, and young boys sopped up blood with dry grass and painted the humps of the remaining camels back in the corral. Two Waata men, invited for the purpose, began to butcher the animal.*

⁂

Several people in a group nearby lifted a figure from among them, a woman, who seemed intoxicated or ill. She was in fact very ill. Her head hung to her chest, so he could not see her face, but as she was moved he could hear her groan over the singing. Her helpers brought her to the fire. Her skinny body was asymmetric, not arranged right. Unless you counted her limbs she seemed more spider than human, carried like that, then laid out on the skin near the fire, straightened out and tidied like tent poles ready for storage. It was Ado's mother. He could see her face now in the firelight, in such discomfort that she seemed to grin.

The singing continued. It grew louder, more intent. People's faces were even, flat. Not indifferent. Not clinical. Not passionate, either. Waiting. Expectant. Their eyes on the fire and the woman near it.

A woman unfastened the sick woman's dress and exposed her chest and belly. A third poured what looked at first like water but dripped in the firelight like oil into Duba's hands, and Duba, sweating, head rollicking to the rhythm of the singing, rubbed his hands together and then drew them across the woman's chest and stomach, over the flat and lifeless breasts, breasts that had given life to children, over the sagging empty flesh of her belly, at which the woman shuddered. A man standing behind Duba stepped forward and offered him a large knife, like a kitchen knife with a wooden handle and a slightly curved blade. It was a knife used for slaughtering animals.

What's he doing? Is he going to cut her or, worse, kill her? Is it euthanasia? Human sacrifice? Savagery? Such things do not happen here, though they have festered for so long in imaginations elsewhere as endemic to this place that even I, trained to debunk such beliefs, think it. It is the first thing that comes to mind. I think it, but I cannot believe it. People do not actually do such things, not anymore. But these are not the usual people: This is Ayana, and Ayana is different. I do not understand Ayana. People I know and trust believe that Ayana is evil.

The singing stops.

Suddenly, the only sound is the crackle of fire and the hush of wind.

Duba stands before the woman, holds the knife over his head, flat, lying on his open hands. The woman beside Ado's mother says words I cannot hear and pours more oil on her torso and it runs smoothly over the lump below her breasts. She lies still, unmoved, exhausted, perhaps even asleep. Other women hold her arms. Are they supporting or restraining her? I cannot say.

Should I do something? But what? I turn to the man beside me, catch his eye in the firelight. The man looks back and shakes his head and returns his gaze to the woman. The other shows no alarm, only a flat disinterest, a student at a lecture. But the man puts his hand out and lays it on my arm. Is this comfort or restraint? I do not know. I turn my own face back to the fire.

Duba makes an incision across the woman's chest and stomach. I nearly scream with her. I want to scream, to stop the performance, but cannot; there is nothing I can do, it is not my business anyway, not my culture, and anyway my cowardice in this moment is larger than my fear. What can I do but invite the same fate upon myself? I shift position. The man's hand tightens, not painfully but firmly. The woman's belly glows bronze in the firelight, and as Duba makes his incision, a trickle of blood flows behind the knife down the slopes and curves of the woman's belly. The incision is long and will leave a scar like that of open heart surgery. My grandfather had that. I cannot say how deep the cut is. There is blood, but there is surprisingly little blood. Is the wound superficial, I wonder, hardly more than a scratch? Are they merely bleeding her?

Then, just as Dasse do when they sacrifice a goat or sheep, they stand and step forward and in turns touch the woman's blood with a finger of their right hands and daub the blood on their foreheads, even the women, who do no such thing at a normal sacrifice. At a normal sacrifice participants take the blood of the victim and in that way share its life. This is different, like the community is taking the sickness, the death of the woman, and sharing it, diffusing its energy among themselves. I cannot imagine that this is a cure, that it even pretends to be, or that it relieves the woman's suffering. Perhaps it is a small respite, to receive these attentions from so many. Perhaps that is all.

It wasn't human sacrifice. Or bleeding.

The knife confused him. The surreal night. The firelight. His imagination.

What happened was this. While the woman anointed Ado's mother with oil, another brought a female sheep to Duba. It was a young ewe, white with black patches. The woman held the sheep's head, and Duba slit its throat in the customary Dasse way, collecting the blood in a milking bowl, others nearby restraining the bucking legs and torso. Duba lifted the blood to his own lips, seemed to take a sip, and dropped to his knees and offered the blood to Ado's mother, dripping some on her chest where it ran in a stream down around the swollen belly. He then lay the bowl beside her, and it was that blood the congregation touched with their fingers and daubed on their foreheads.

What led him to think that Duba's knife was intended for Ado's mother? What led him to believe they would do such a thing?

Perhaps it was the dark imaginings of centuries.

Perhaps it was the way of all sacrifices, the use of scapegoats, to create confusion about the object.

Perhaps it was the way of symbolism, to muddy the space between symbol and symbolized.

He was now thinking like an anthropologist. The thinking distanced him, comforted him, and he knew that that was the point of it, to remove himself. Rationality could not go there, not all the way.

He did not step forward to daub his own finger in the blood and himself with it.

Ado's mother seemed relaxed, asleep. The woman who had stood by her refastened her dress and laid a cloth across her, a man's clean white sheet.

AS THE TWO *Waata men butchered the camel, friends of the dead man's sons shaved their heads and placed new thorn branches as doors in the openings of the old man's corrals. The sons were now independent of their father. The* angafa, *the eldest son, inherits his father's livestock. But he also inherits obligations: He must give his father's brother a camel because whoever inherits the spear also gets a camel. And he must honor the gifts of livestock his father made to other sons, their* guma. *But lines are blurry. If brothers remain together after the death of their father, the eldest acts as head of the family, so they may leave their animals in his* boma. *If they wish to leave, they may also do so after* sorio hamtu, *taking their animals with them.*

⁂

Duba, standing, shouted the line of a new song, and the others answered in song. They returned to their singing and dancing. He remained, moving now, if only slightly, to the rhythms, unable to leave, unable fully to participate: sitting, watching.

He thought, if the sick woman were helped at all by the ceremony, the benefit derived, at least in part, from the attention of the group. Her whole society was present, dancing, sitting, witnessing, focusing their eyes on her: She was receptacle, receiver. Perhaps the cure, if there was one, lay in the act of submission. What normally occurred at Ayana rites, near as he could tell from what he'd been told and what he'd read, was that an afflicted person, usually a woman, would dance, along with others, and eventually be possessed, and then a medium, a figure like Duba, would talk with the spirit and find out what it wanted. The woman would talk, but it was the spirit who occupied her that did the talking. In that way they discerned what would cure the woman, or at least ease the symptoms. In this rite, however, the afflicted could not speak, let alone dance. But that didn't seem to matter. The group danced for her. The group bathed her with its attention. Perhaps in that way the spirit felt addressed and would—one could only hope—ease the pain. The woman gave herself to Duba and the others, and there must have been some release, some relaxation, some peace that came with that.

He thought of his wife, who had found a sort of happiness not by submitting herself to his life on the desert but by accepting a life, a compromise, nearby. That was art. It was accepting the constraints placed on a canvas by the previous marks—each mark conditioning what came next. It was not the artist's will that made the art as much as her ability to work with what presented itself.

Submission did not come easily. Despite his willingness to live with other people, more or less on their terms, he could not give up himself. He watched. He rolled his body with the rhythms of what the people were singing. He did not know the words, but that did not matter. He knew the melody, expressed it with gasp and groan. He moved his shoulders as the others moved theirs, lost himself in song, at least as far as he was able. In the end he could not let go, not completely. He didn't have the skill to give himself over to the present.

He began to weep. He was not sure when it began. At some point he noticed his face was wet. He was unsure what he wept for. His uncertainty alarmed him, the sudden inscrutable appearance of tears. Perhaps it was her. But which her? Perhaps it was everything. Perhaps it was his sense of not belonging. Not there. Not anywhere. Not anymore.

NOW THE CROWD *that had gathered for* sorio hamtu *ate meat. First the liver was roasted, cut into small pieces, and distributed to all: Everyone must get at least a taste of the liver. Then, while women boiled the meat, others cut slabs of hump fat,* gobo, *into cubes, and these were distributed all around and eaten raw or skewered on sticks and saved to be taken home. The fat was firm and white and sweet, like the fat of beefsteak. The meat and fat of the camel's right side was the share of the* d'abella. *They would eat this that day and the next within the* hos. *The front left leg was the young men's share, and they took it far away from camp, to a distant tree, and roasted it themselves apart from the elders. The rear left leg belonged to the family. The neck was the brother's wife's. The left side of the hump was* dandama, *for all to share; it was the slab cubed and distributed.*

People lingered for several hours, eating meat and fat, visiting, sleeping in slivers of shade. Still there were no prayers.

The next morning the d'abella *would drink* buna*—a concoction of whole coffee berries, fried to a char in butter, and swimming in a mix of sweetened hot milk and oil—and pray, officially lifting* hamtu *from the family.*

⁂

He didn't remember leaving. He must have left before the others. He had an image of that: but had he reconstructed it or did he remember? He was still convinced of the difference, even as he woke in the morning. He thought of himself sifting his way into the dark, released by the crowd. Perhaps sent away. Perhaps one of them led him away just as one of them had brought him in. Perhaps his gaze was too much, his difference, his looking on. He drifted up the hillside to the path, took path to road, road to settlement, and somehow found the old man's house. He must have. How could it have been otherwise? He did not remember whether he had difficulty finding the house in the dark.

He woke to wind and pale thin light leaking through cracks at the metal seams, woke to smoke from the granddaughter's fire, woke to crusted snot in nostrils and eyes, woke to a vague location between sleeping and waking, a place in which to linger over the large and innocuous. He lingered over the woman in the night and thought about his wife, and the two women settled into his morning brain as one: the frailty, the weakness, the sagging deflated look in their eyes, the pain, the hope in some sort of turn, a miracle. And he thought that bleeding her might have helped, the laying on of hands, the attention, and then he thought it could only have hurt, like massaging an unset broken bone. And he thought, what were Duba and the others thinking? He woke to another sense of himself as well. Knew enough to check. The soles of his feet, inured to the sandals and walking, less pained than they'd been when he arrived at Abudo's camp, felt stiff and dirty but strong. He felt relief in his chest, emptiness, like a demon had been unreined and let go and run off like an animal and was gone now and grazing somewhere at the edge of things.

He woke to resolution, decision.

He would go. If you asked he could not have said where or why, which was curious because, if you'd asked about somebody else's aims, as an anthropologist, he'd have offered an opinion. That was the outsider's advantage, the privilege of the other. He had only the knowledge that he was not ready to go home. He knew that. That was what he woke to: He would not stay, he would not go home. Instead, drawing on a certainty he could not have explained, arising from he knew not where, he'd go north, alone, into the frontier, across the border, onto the escarpment there, to a place where he could camp and think and submit himself to what he had done and not done, to what they had done and not done. And in that way find—what? Cure? Relief? The end of his journey? Then perhaps he would go home. It was no good going home before he was ready.

The granddaughter cracked branches in her small fists and fed the fire beneath the pot. She boiled water and added tea leaves and sugar to it and poured the strong black over-sweet tea into a large tin cup and served the *ferenji*. Then she served Ali, who rose, a ghost under his sheet, and took the cup with an outstretched hand. Then the old man, sitting up the while on his bed chewing tobacco, staring into nothing, filled with memories, or so he assumed, reliving a life, not needing nor wanting anything new.

He and Ali murmured greetings to each other and adjusted themselves to the new morning. No one spoke of the night before. Ali seemed nonetheless to know and understand. Ali accepted without surprise, without need of explanation, his instructions to return the camels to his father. Ali, of course, would return by way of Toricha and his girlfriend. The *ferenji* would continue alone, not to Balessa, as planned, not yet, but north to Forole, then beyond, into the frontier, across the border, and up the escarpment on the other side. He wanted time. Time away. Time without anybody or anything. Without. Without these people. Without his people. Without. Without. The word repeated itself in his head until it was not the lack of something, like going without, but the location of something: not within but without, elsewhere, gone.

Ali asked the girl for hot water and she brought it in a basin and he took it to the porch and bathed his face and hair and hands.

He followed suit with fresh water. He splashed the warm soapless water on his face and rubbed it in his eyes and scrubbed the dust from the nape of his neck and the hollows of his ears. He gazed out over the town through the fog and pale light, like looking through skimmed milk or onion skin, shadows only, and he did not know how to begin, how to take the first step, what he would need, what exactly he was going to do when he got there, knowing only that he had to go.

The camels were up on three legs and in this hobbled state had hopped to a bush that grew behind the house and were nibbling the leaves, nodding their heads at each other, as if they were trying to shake off the sleep of a bad night.

The man who had pulled him into the crowd was named Gollo. With Ali's help, he found Gollo's homestead, and with Gollo's help they found a family that would sell a donkey. He did not think he could handle a camel alone, and a camel would not be healthy where he was going, not for long. There were too many ticks and attendant diseases at elevations above the desert floor. He didn't know how long he'd be gone, and he didn't want to have Ali or anybody else with him. Besides, he liked the idea of traveling simply, peasant style, with a burro. It was an old nag, healthy but compliant, which was just what he needed.

They returned with the donkey to the old man's house. He set aside his gear: clothes, sleeping sheet, one of the cow skins, cooking supplies, two of the four plastic jerry cans still full of brown water from the Toricha *lagga*, and an old two-liter plastic vegetable-oil jug as canteen. He and Ali loaded the burro with all this and loaded the camels with what remained. The granddaughter came out and watched but did not offer to help. She might not have known how, growing up atop Badda Hurri, a place inhospitable to camels. She said nothing. Her grandfather called, and she retreated. They finished loading. They'd learned how in the time they'd been together. That much they'd accomplished. He thought the big man, Duba, would have arrived before now, that he would decide what they should do, or at least present them with an edge against which to work, but Duba did not show up.

He rubbed his hands together to shake off the dirt and looked around. He'd arrived only the night before. So little had changed and so much.

The town was foggy and vague, asleep. It was too cold for early morning labors on the thin farms. They tied the loaded camels and burro to the porch and returned inside. They said *nagayat* to the old man and his granddaughter, who was in the kitchen, and she emerged and handed them small bundles covered in newspaper, each a clutch of chapatis. He was relieved to have the flat bread for the journey, for it would have been a long day to walk with nothing but strong tea on his stomach. He gave the old man a couple of large handfuls of tobacco. The man's face lit up with pleasure, the first he'd shown. He answered their *nagayat* with *nagayat*, spit off the side of his bed, and looked at the wall.

They left. Ali turned south, he north. The old man did not emerge. Ali disappeared into the fog.

He saw no one as he led the burro out of town, except one man returning from checking his field.

EVERY YEAR AFTER *the camel sacrifice—indeed, every time a member of the family passes the grave—relatives make an offering of tobacco and* megado, *coffee beans if they have them, and perhaps a libation of milk. Then, eight years after the death, the family returns to the grave to sweep it: scattering what remains of the man's or woman's belongings from the pile into the wind and pulling the rocks down and tossing them away from the grave. If circumstances make it difficult for the family to gather for* iresa haran *after eight years, they may do so after sixteen years. Sweeping the grave after eight or sixteen years links the event with age-grade cycles, emphasizing a connection between dead and surviving generations. The memory of the dead is not gone but faded. Family members no longer have an obligation to offer tobacco when they pass, though they may do so. Sweeping the grave, an event I never saw, though I saw its effects, leaves a reversed, or negative, image of the grave in its place: Where there was a large rock cairn with bare ground around it, there is now a circular clearing surrounded by a ring of rocks.*

XXII

Gollo, the man who helped him buy the donkey, warned against making the journey alone. He assumed Gollo worried he could not walk so far. Dasse were doubtful that *ferenji*, who typically rode places in Land Rovers, were capable of walking long distances. In fact, Gollo was worried about lions. He advised him to make camp early, gather enough firewood to last the night, and build a corral of thorn branches around the edge of his camp—all of which would take a lone man several hours. He would make one camp on the way to Forole, spend a night at Forole, replenish his water, then set out for another two-day walk north onto the escarpment. It was the second of these journeys that presented the most risk, for it was wilder, less populated, less known to him, and there were more lions there than on Badda Hurri.

He found himself walking along a road for the first time in weeks. It wasn't much of a road. No traffic. Just a track used by the odd lorry that passed, in a busy period, once every couple of weeks. It was smoothed-over dirt, graded at one time, cleared of brush. Parts of it had washed out God knows when and resembled a creek bed. The road turned to avoid rock outcroppings and switched back and forth as it dropped to the scrubby lowlands below. No vehicle without good clearance and four-wheel drive would have managed it, and even then it was slow going. He remembered this from before when a lorry driver carrying relief food let him ride along to Forole. That lorry had been built like a tank to traverse the roughest country, and even it had had to creep along in places. For most of the first day, once the clouds lifted, the elevation gave him a view of the lowlands north across the national border. Below he could see the road straighten to a tangent aimed at Mount Forole, a pale shadow on the horizon. Having walked on narrow paths for the past month the road, such as it was, seemed excessive, like an abandoned highway, and he caught himself now and then drifting to one side and then the other, unsure with all the space how to keep a straight path. He went north because it was away, the direction he least wanted to go, not back to what he was, but off toward something else, toward change, toward difference, toward her. She wasn't here. She was elsewhere.

He would go elsewhere.

❖

She was never out of his mind. Yet until the Ayana night she had not, for some time, been forefront. She'd shifted. The distinction between her and everything else softened. He could think of her, reassemble her, if he wanted. But she was in all that he saw, everything he did. It was all her, and none of it was her exactly. When he thought of her she was healthy, she was herself; the illness wasn't her, it was a sucking away of her. Ado's mother had brought her to mind in a new and startling way. The woman on the cow skin, the helpless tangle of arms and legs, the gaunt face, vacant eyes and long teeth, had taken him fiercely back to the last months at home, when she'd lost everything but breath.

She no longer held him, could no longer grasp. When he carried her to the bathroom for toilet or bath, her arm fell across his shoulder like an empty sleeve. She was thin beyond anorexia, thin as a spider. Bed sheets clung to her bones like cobwebs. Then he gave up carrying her to the bath. The pain and disruption were too great. She could not tell him. He simply guessed. He bathed her in bed with a washcloth, changed the sheets after. It was only when it was too late that he wondered whether he should have let go sooner. The idea was absurd. There it was. Should he have ended her suffering? They'd never spoken of it. Then she'd been unable to say, he unable to know. She could only stare with eyes blank and rheumy and silent. Her eyes, once so clear and focused, now said nothing he knew how to read. Once again he'd held on, wanting her to stay with him, preferring the small warmth of a silent body, her silent body, the uncertain gaze, the raspy breath, to nothing. Even as there was so little else, as she suffered the daily indignities of total dependence, he held on—lovingly, steadfastly, selfishly.

⁂

He stopped once to let the donkey graze. He ate a piece of flat bread and some of what remained of the dried meat from Toricha. In the afternoon he walked on to the plain, along the straightened road toward Forole. Its engineers had drawn a bead on the distant mountain and simply plowed a line. The country was scrubby, full of low-lying trees, more bushes than trees, and more of them than on the other side of Badda Hurri. It was country easy to get lost in but for the road, and easy to hide in. If he'd been someone to worry about bandits, now would have been the time to worry, but he wasn't—the road simply wasn't trafficked enough to warrant a bandit's waiting. He saw hardly any game: Once, a secretary bird, large as an eagle with long terrestrial legs, walked across the road ahead. He startled a pair of giraffes foraging treetops. They retreated into the brush. There were small birds, like long-tailed sparrows, and a few sand grouse that he admired as they darted above.

He quit at four, giving himself two hours before dark to build a fence of thorn branches and collect firewood for the night. He tied a rope between the unloaded donkey's front legs and let it hobble where it would while he worked. Cutting branches and firewood was hot work. The air was much warmer than atop the mountain. He pricked himself on the thorns and bled a good bit and got himself quite dirty with dust and sweat. Afterward he bathed in the dusky light, using precious water, and drank as much as he wanted. Cooled from the bath, he lit a fire. He did not bother to cook but heated water for tea, ate a cold chapati and the last of the dried Toricha meat. He rummaged in his pack for the notebook and pen and, moved by the silence more than anything, began to write for the first time since he'd left home. In fact, for the first time since her death.

On my own. Ali has returned to Maikona by way of Elema's camp. Seems strange not to have him around. And freeing. For a month we've shared meals, more than a hundred miles of walking, the same cow skin for bed. We were traveling companions, not friends. I am, I suppose, too old. My language isn't good enough. And maybe he was fearful, intimidated. I don't fit any of the usual categories. For some reason Abudo and I hit it off, even at the beginning when there was no language between us. We just liked each other. I was different. We had more in common.

I call the donkey Dapple, the name of Quixote's horse. The donkey *cost me the equivalent of $50. He's old and gray with rough prickly coat and muzzle soft as an earlobe. The contrast is interesting. Also the smell. More horse than camel. A camel is more cow than horse and so's the smell. Dapple's solid, obedient. I don't have to chase him all over the countryside, just point him and he walks. He pretty much has one speed.*

Walking with the donkey is different from walking with camels: different pace, different rhythm. Camels stride unhurriedly and while they're not hard to keep up with they don't dawdle. The donkey takes so many more steps: seems to be in a hurry, but creeps along. His pace is slower than a camel's. Sound is different, too. Camels sway slowly to and fro and the sound of the jerry cans sloshing up there reminds me of the sea, like a boat swaying in waves. The donkey with its staccato steps makes the water sound like a bartender shaking a drink. It is funny and I find myself smiling, walking behind him. Dapple has such a flat slow personality and he's funny. Go figure.

I'm doing something different, something you'd admire: following my footsteps north. I'm going to camp and lie low and avoid people and, well, I don't know: think, feel, be. I'm going to try. I can't think what else to do. What do you think? What would you do?

The morning on the mountain was cold and foggy. Thick fog. You could see the ground but that was it. Otherwise, white. Milk white. I guess it's not fog but cloud. Spooky: someone would walk up in the mist and appear like a ghost out of nothing, and when they walked away they disappeared the same. Evaporated. When the wind's blowing you can't hear their footsteps. Fog clears by midmorning, though, and then it's sunny until middle afternoon, sometimes clear straight through. I remember that from before.

The man named Gollo who helped me find the donkey gave me a spear for the journey. Said I should have a spear if I'm alone. Abudo gave me a walking stick for the same reason. A man's got to have something to poke around with. Gollo warned of lions. Pastoralists always worry about predators. Still, I am alone. Saw no one all day.

I have a sack of chapatis that the granddaughter of the old man Ali and I stayed with gave me. And some dried meat. No milk. Sugar and tea leaves. In Forole, there'll be milk to buy and maybe a few onions and potatoes.

No fog down here. Badda Hurri behind is clouded up. So is Forole in front. Saw sand grouse flying in from somewhere. Maikona? All that way? Fast. Like jets. On the way also saw giraffes and zebra, grazing in the distance. One secretary bird. Several vultures. And a bird, I can't remember its name, with long tail, like a single feather that's three times the body's length or more: a tit with really long tail.

⁂

They'd debated, anthropologist and painter, about subjectivity and objectivity. It was in the nature of their different disciplines—hers softer, impressionistic; his harder, less personal, a science of sorts. She told him once that accuracy mattered very little. He remembered the conversation on his journey onto the plains north of Badda Hurri. It was years into their marriage, but they were young still and talked endlessly about everything. They were in the car on a cross-country vacation. He drove. The seat between them was littered with gum wrappers, cigarette packs, and empty cups of coffee.

What does accuracy do, she said, except verify you've been somewhere? If you were actually there, does it matter that you can prove it? It doesn't make a painting or story truer.

He didn't understand, so she explained with an analogy.

Suppose, she said, you're on a road trip. Like this. She gestured out the window. As you travel, you play a game, finding words on road signs whose first letters correspond in order with letters of the alphabet. It's a common game. You look for a word beginning with A; when you find it you look for a word beginning with B. *Arizona. Buckle. Clarksville. Detour. Exit.* And so on.

You keep track of the words, she said. Turn it into a memory game. The list of words, in alphabetical order, forms a code for that stretch of highway. They're its fingerprint. The sequence of words describes a stretch of road unlike any other. And if you include words on the sides of trucks and tractor-trailers, well, it's not only unique to that stretch but also to that moment.

What's the point? he asked.

That's the point, she answered. The sequence is accurate for a particular time and place. But what does it tell you? Nothing. Nonsense. A list of words in alphabetical order. It's just a sequence. There are thousands, millions, billions of different sequences. There's no end to them. You could come up with the sequence of insects from one place to another, or the genders of people you pass along the way, or which hands people walk around with in their pockets. In out out in in in out. If you want accuracy, you can get it all sorts of ways. What does it give you? It only tells someone else who already knows the sequence that you were there, saw it, too. So what?

That's too easy, he said, winding up his window to ease the wind in his ears. It's nonsense if you pick a nonsense sequence. If you observe the cars and trucks that pass along a road, that actually tells you something interesting about the road: A road in one part of the world is different from roads in other parts of the world, has different traffic.

You still have a list, she said. The list of signs is interesting, too, if you're interested in the types of words people put on signs in a particular part of the world. It's really no different.

What I think is interesting, she went on, is that for the list to be interesting you have to bring something else to it. You have to *want* what's on it, and that isn't a matter of accuracy. It's not about the place but about you. If you happen to want a list of cars, then a list of cars is interesting—an accurate list even more so. But the accuracy doesn't make it interesting. It's what you think, what you want, that makes it interesting. And what you think is something you've made up, not something there to begin with.

That may be true in your business, he said. But in mine the point is you were there, you actually saw what you write about, and for that you have to prove you were there. If you make it up, you lose the actuality, you lose the point.

Do you? she wondered. What do you lose? I don't believe people look at paintings or read books, even in your business, just because they're accurate. They look at paintings because they like what they show. They read books because they like what they say. Of course, they must have some relation to the world. But it needn't line up exactly. Even if it does line up, the lining up doesn't make it a good representation of the place. What do the words in the order of the alphabet tell you about the stretch of road you've passed? Or the list of cars that pass along that road? Or the phone numbers in a telephone book? Telephone books have to be among the most accurate books ever printed. But unless you need a number, who wants to read one?

No, for that, she said, you need to make it up. No one would buy my paintings simply because they were accurate. They buy my paintings because they like what I choose to put in them and what I choose to leave out. They like what I make up.

Well, I'm not a painter.

No, you're an anthropologist. We're not so different. We're both trying to make a picture, a representation, of the world and the people in it as near as we can to the way we see it. We can't represent the world itself. What we make isn't the world, it's what we make of it. All we represent is what we see. And that's not a matter of accuracy. Not really. That's a matter of choice and selection and accident. The truth of our representations is mixed up with what we bring to them. I don't believe we can leave out our subjectivities, not and have the truth.

You're playing fast and loose with the words. You're using *accuracy* in a very narrow sense.

Then you pick the word. I'm just saying that objectivity, total non-fiction, doesn't leave you with much that people would want to look at. People already have reality to look at. They don't want more reality.

He disliked what she said. He loved the conversation. Loved her for it. What she said was exciting and strange. Different from anything he'd ever thought. That was what he loved. She was so different. It didn't matter that they disagreed. Listening to her was like falling into an icy stream on a hot day. The intimacy between them had nothing to do with accuracy. He missed talking with her more than anything.

Long frightening night. It was quiet. Firelight lit the fence walls and surrounding bushes, the tree in the enclosure, and several at some distance. Beyond these was blackness. Dapple grunted and woke me from the thin sleep I'd fallen into. He was dancing and looking around nervously. That got me up, heart thumping. I put more wood on the fire and made a calculation about whether we'd collected enough for the night. The spear lay at my side. Dapple eventually relaxed some and I lay back down, conscious of every twitch of sound from beyond the fire ring. A fire centers you like nothing else: you are at the fire and the center of things, and you can see and know what's there but vision dims as you get farther from the fire and then it's just blackness. Looking out I saw two eyes reflected back at me. They held mine, or so it seemed, for a few seconds, and then they began to jiggle and move across the plain and away. They were small. Probably a jackal's.

I woke again between three and four, and the fire had died down a good bit. It was the quiet time before the morning winds. There were still flames but they were small and the fire was mainly hot coals. I built the fire back up, stepped to the edge of the brush fence to pee, and returned. I sensed something was looking, watching us. But wasn't that predictable? I sat on the skin, wrapped in my bed cloth, spear beside me, ready, and looked into the blackness and saw nothing. And again nothing. And nothing again. And then a breath. It was no more than that, barely a sound. A gray blur in my peripheral vision. An owl swung upward into the branch of the nearby tree and perched there and looked our way: big thing, big as an eagle, all gray in the firelight but for two black eyes in the center of dish-sized rims. It perched there for twenty minutes. At least it seemed like twenty minutes. We looked at each other. So I imagined. Then it fell forward and, as it fell, spread its wings and glided into the darkness. Into my darkness. I doubt it was dark for the owl.

When I went out to shit this morning, I found lion tracks. Each print larger than my full-spread hand. No idea how long they'd been there. Not long. Could have been last night. Glad I had a fire.

⁂

He and the donkey arrived in the full heat of afternoon. Forole was no bigger than Badda Hurri, smaller if anything: five or six iron-sheet sheds, a few wattled structures, a dozen Dasse tents, all built on loose sand amid a grove of trees near the base of a mountain with the same name. Here the track from Badda Hurri met another that linked Torbi in the east to Dukana in the west and roughly followed the international border. The Badda Hurri road jogged west along this road for a hundred yards and then turned north across the boundary. The town was a border outpost—little more than a chief with a two-way radio and a few armed askaris. Their presence attracted nomads looking for a reason to settle, a sense of security, who settled here probably because of the chief's meager resources, or maybe they knew him. A couple of small shops, or *maduka*, sold razor blades and flashlight batteries, cloth, rice, flour, sugar, tea leaves, and tobacco, and since he was lucky today, a box full of wrinkled vegetables—potatoes, onions, garlic, even a couple of cabbages—all of which would keep a few days or weeks without refrigeration. There was no natural water nearby, but a water tank, under the chief's control, rigged up as a trailer, was available. It was filled every week or so at wells north of Torbi and supplied the residents of Forole with the water they needed. The chief's building was obvious. In front stood a flagpole and flag surrounded by a ring of white-painted rocks, like flagpoles at official posts throughout the country. The chief, he learned, was away, along with the guards. They'd gone by way of Torbi to Marsabit, the district office, and weren't expected back for a month. The young man who told him all this invited him to his mother's iron-sheet house nearby. She made tea and, that evening, dinner from the potatoes and onions and rice he'd bought, and the three of them ate together. He tethered Dapple to a post beside the house and bedded down on his skin nearby. As he drifted off he heard familiar sounds from inside, whispered voices telling stories, the clatter of pots, laughter, and then it was just the wind. Now and then he was wakened by a passing figure, the sound of feet on soft sandy earth. Someone off to visit a lover, perhaps, or rendezvous with a friend. There was no fire to tend. All was darkness and starlight. He was back in a camp, of sorts, a fixed camp with permanent walls and roofs. He was safe. He was also anxious. His body, cramped and stiff, wanted to move, to leave the place as soon as light allowed. The place reminded him of Badda Hurri without the veiling mist.

◈

I find it almost impossible not to think. Anthropology purports to offer access to other people and their ways. Techniques and theory. In fact, anthropology gets in the way. Truth is we cannot have it both ways. Thinking as an anthropologist holds me back, prevents me from understanding. I have to laugh. There I was during the Ayana night singing and dancing, wanting to lose myself in that moment, to be with them and thereby to conjure the spirits—I can't believe I just wrote those words. Yet my awareness *of what was happening, my* intention *to have those experiences, my* consciousness *of it all, to notice what they were doing so I could do it, too, all that guaranteed my failure actually to do it.*

My students ask how anthropologists avoid having an effect on the people they study. They fix on that idea, that the observer changes the observed. Of course they do. But our effect on them is not such a big deal. I have a new insight about this. It isn't so much that anthropologists affect others and therefore get biased data. It's that we can't escape ourselves. Our consciousness gets in our way, not theirs. Our questions, our thinking about what is going on, our writing up our answers—all of it blows us farther and farther away from where we want to go, from what they are doing, from what we ourselves are doing. Think about it. I can be here or I can think about being here. But I can't be both—the one is a remove from the other. They may be close. They are close. But they are not the same. All of my work, all of the things I've written, all of it has described people in some sense, has been about them, has been in a sense true, more or less accurate, but it has not been them. As an old anthropologist said, the map is not the territory. We lose sight of that. Well, we do and we don't. We nod to it. Then we write up everything as if the texts actually get it, as if they matter. As much as we love our theories, our capacity to be conscious of what we do, we forget that our descriptions are word by word leading us away from the very thing we want—at least I want—which is to enter the experience of another, to bridge the space between us. It is too confusing to write. But isn't that what any of us wants—whether we're anthropologists or not—to merge with others, families, friends, lovers, whole villages? Strip down and crawl right in. Lose ourselves. Close the gap. End the separation. Have that. That is what urges us on, isn't it? To connect and experience humanity in some new and fresh and original way. Yet our intention to do so, our trying to be thoughtful about how best to do it, so that we are careful and not deluding ourselves, that very method, that rigor, just creates a boundary between us. All I wanted was to sing and dance and share the delight and seriousness of that night, and my desire to do so, a desire which arose from the differences between us, my incapacity, my lack of understanding, was the very thing that held me back. I cannot move faster than my own tail, can never quite catch it. Not that way. Don't say I told you so. I admit it. I learned this from you. The only way to get somewhere, really, is by indirection, not to try.

He rose early and crossed the border at dawn. No one knew his plans. The boy and mother asked. He was vague. He told them he wanted to visit friends north of Forole. They asked who, and he gave them names of people he knew were camped somewhere north of the border: Ramat Funan and his son, Jillo. Names of people they did not happen to know, but it would have been all right if they had known. They urged him not to go alone. The border was marked by concrete and stone obelisks painted white and set at intervals of about fifty or a hundred yards. The border was virtually unpatrolled by either side. As far as the two capitals were concerned, the region was a no-man's land.

Chief Boru was what patrol there was for his side, and he wasn't around. He counted on the same attitude on the other. But the obelisks made it nearly impossible to claim he didn't know what he was doing. What was the worst they would do? He doubted they'd shoot a *ferenji* traveling with a donkey. They'd stop him. They might even throw him in jail for a few days. In the end, though, they'd probably send him back south.

The bush was dense, green, full of tall shrubs and short trees, nothing much taller than ten feet. It was a flat land with occasional hills, remnants of volcanoes millions of years old. The hills, rare and random, seemed artificial in their oddity, like burial mounds, like something put there by ancient people. None was much more than hundreds of feet tall. Huge overgrown eroded pyramids. You could climb one in an hour and get a look-see. They were covered in scree and boulders and shrubs and little else. Still, some, he knew, were sacred, marking points of the mythical origin of Dasse clans. Here was the garden of Eden, the place where God, in the beginning of beginnings, set everything in motion.

He knew from before that the road led north from Forole to a fork. From there it continued northeast up the escarpment toward Melbanna then due north again to Mega; a path, the other prong of the fork, followed a *lagga* north to a spring at the base of the escarpment. He had never been to the spring but knew the fork and when he reached it turned the donkey along the path toward the spring. From the fork he could see the escarpment clearly, a blue-gray wall of steep mountain and cliff roughly ten miles ahead running east-west as far as his eye could see. His plan was to follow its grade up, about midway. He knew that the escarpment was not as steep or steady as it looked from a distance, that there were ledges and plateaus along the slopes where he could make camp, from which he'd have a view south of the country he'd walked through. He hoped to reach the spring by late afternoon, climb the escarpment the next day.

The spring was an oasis, cool and succulent, forested by tall dome palms and large acacias, green and vibrant from the strangely moist and fertile earth. A clear space of sand and clay showed signs of livestock come to water, but when he arrived late in the day the place was deserted. Beside an ancient thorn tree, thick and black and graceful as live oak, limbs sprawling low and parallel to the earth rather than reaching upward, was a shallow pool of clear dark water, fed from a spring among a pile of boulders set against the slope of the escarpment. The old limbs of the tree were low enough to be climbed and sat upon, and the bark in those places was worn smooth and brown. A troop of baboons waded at the bank of the pool. One male screeched to see him, and they all dashed into the brush. He did not see them again. He hobbled the donkey and fashioned a new corral from an old one already cut by a previous traveler, supplementing it with new branches. The spring was sure to attract game and predators. He gathered firewood, bathed beside the pool, the bottom of which was black with rocks and algae, built a fire, prepared tea, made a stew of onions and potatoes, and was asleep with darkness.

Dapple woke me with a snort. He was stomping the ground where he was tethered by the fence gate, head held in place by the halter but back swaying to and fro. Could have trampled me. The gate was nothing more than a gap in the thorn fence with a single spreading branch pulled in front. The donkey's snorting sounded like he was trying to clear a burr from his nose. I'd been sound asleep and was startled.

First thing I sat up, grabbed my electric torch and pointed it out beyond the fence. Nothing but darkness, gray where the torchlight fell, black everywhere else but on the few trees and nearby bushes, which were rusty orange in the firelight. The donkey paused, alert to my sudden alertness, and I listened and heard nothing but some hissing from the fire. There was no wind. It was somewhere in the hours after midnight when the wind quits. Dapple resumed prancing. I feared he'd pull the fence apart, but I didn't want to set him loose either, for he would have run all over and there wasn't much room.

I figured hyenas. They are the most likely because they're the most numerous and they get their noses into things. But if they were close they weren't showing themselves and I didn't figure they would slink about so much. I've often seen hyenas lingering at the periphery of camps, eyes blazing from the torch light. And there were those hyenas that attacked Elema's camp. But nothing now. Just darkness and trees.

Then I saw the lion's face, or part of it. It was like one of those optical quizzes where you have to look at a dazzling pattern in just the right way to see the code, which, when your focus is right, emerges suddenly into view and then you can't see anything else.

The lion was crouched to the left of a bush about twenty yards beyond the fence. I found that I could even smell it, a musky odor, a mix of vinegar and dust, like lions I've smelled at circuses, only fainter. Perhaps I imagined that.

The only thing showing was the top half of its head, its eyes, its forehead and short mane. Its ears were drawn back and I couldn't see them. When I shined my torch light on it the head dipped a little lower so I could barely make out the eyes.

I thought then and belatedly how little protection the thorn fence provided against a lion. Perhaps hyenas would be deterred by it, or at least slowed enough that I might rise, shine a light, poke at them with the spear. But what could I do with a lion, which was perfectly capable of leaping over the fence?

Why hadn't it jumped already? The fire?

I held the torch on the face, or tried to, while I added sticks to the fire, built it up, collected the spear and stood, saying soothing words to Dapple, who wasn't snorting anymore but was worried, flanks quivering.

Thank God I gathered as much wood as I did. Still I wondered whether I'd have enough for the rest of the night. Eventually I could burn the fence. What time was it? It was two o'clock. The moon was gone. The lion was still there. Crouched. Waiting.

I read somewhere that gazelles graze within sight of lions, preferring to have their enemy near. As long as they know where the lion is and what the lion is doing, however close, they can get away if it charges. A gazelle can outrun a lion. Lions apparently don't charge except by surprise. I wondered if the rule applied to humans and donkeys. I waited.

I thought for a time about how to use the spear. I've carried spears, but never actually used one. I knew enough not to throw it but to use it like a sword, held forth, to impale whatever attacked. I wondered what I would do with a second lion? I prayed there was no second lion.

In the thick of it I became aware of myself being thankful that you were not there, thinking oddly that you were safe, wherever you were. Safe from what? I'm not sure. From this? From life? From me? At the same time I wished you had been there, to see it, a tableau of a certain sort, a painting lit by firelight, a scene as old as humanity. You'd have been thrilled. The first people probably learned to use fire not so much to cook with but to keep predators away. They must have stoked the fire through the night, waited up watching, making sure the fire worked. How could anyone sleep with a lion waiting at the fall line of light? Of course, the first humans had others with them. They'd have seldom if ever traveled alone, so they had company to support them, watch their backs, look in the other directions where other faces might be lurking, who might stab at the second lion if another charged.

The lion lingered. Dapple shivered. We all waited. The fire faded. I added wood.

It felt like an hour but was only ten or fifteen minutes. The lion must have begun to relax for suddenly its ears popped up. I say suddenly. I don't know if they came up all of a sudden. It could have been my attention. One moment I noticed they were up. The head rose a little. I saw that. I could almost see its whole face, there beyond the stones and grass, beside the low bush, its body still out of view.

Then the lion shook its head, as if to stir away a fly, though at night there probably wasn't a fly, and it grunted and yawned: Bored? Tense? I have no idea. It stood up, then sat, licked a paw, continued to sit, looking remarkably like a cat, a large cat, with no expression except itself, a flat regard, without attachment: the dangerous look of a Buddha, neither interested nor uninterested. It grunted, rose to all fours, and walked the long way around camp. I followed with the torch, heart pounding for fear that the lion was searching for the place from which to leap, the right angle, that the lion was toying with me. It kept walking, out past the brush, out past the firelight, out past the reach of the torch, into the black night, leaving me wide awake with much of the night left to count my blessings.

⁂

The lion's visit held his attention the rest of the night and into the next day. He felt he'd come close to the edge of something. He knew that had it attacked he would not have been able to fend the beast off, that luck alone left him alive. He was puzzled by his reaction. The lion had frightened, but it also thrilled. He was unsure what to make of the combination. Throughout his journey he had felt dogged by a threat that never materialized. Perhaps the danger wasn't chasing him as much as he was chasing it. He was frightened and excited by the lion, titillated in fact by the prospect of the journey ending, reaching some conclusion. It surprised him to think of such an ending: He was a little disappointed that the lion hadn't attacked.

There were few lions on the desert. It was too dry to sustain sufficient game to support large numbers of territorial lions. The livestock, which were numerous, were also well defended. There were more lions on the greener mountains, where kudu and buffalo and other, smaller ungulates grazed, and the lions enjoyed green foliage to hide in and spring from.

Years before, he had met an eighty-one-year-old man at Maikona, then recovering from a lion attack. His story was well known. He was famous among Dasse. He heard the story several times, from the old man himself as well as others, and always it was the same story. Dasse were not given to exaggeration. The old man, a couple sons, and a few other young men had been tending cattle in the Marsabit forest. A lion appeared before dark one evening and sprang upon the back of one of the heifers. The young men fled, but the old man refused to abandon his stock. He dropped his staff, unsheathed his knife, and charged. The lion growled angrily, swatted at the irritation, then abandoned the heifer and leapt upon the man. As the old man went down he offered his left hand to the lion's mouth and grabbed its tongue, which, he said later, was rough as stone. It turned out to be a brilliant strategy. With the knife in his other hand, and the lion's mouth occupied, he slashed its throat and the blood spilled over him, bathing him in wet warmth. The lion relaxed its three hundred pounds on him and pinned him so he could barely breathe. Eventually the younger men summoned their courage and returned. They pushed the lion's body off their father. Doctors at the hospital refused to sew up the wounds for fear of infection. They bathed and swaddled the gashes and punctures, which were many, especially on the one arm, and pumped him full of antibiotics. For the rest of his life he would look as if he'd been crudely glued together. He didn't mind. Each scar was a medal. He got special care. The hospital, for lack of medicine and staff, could be indifferent to patients. But not to a lion killer. The old man was a hero. He pretty much had to live. How could he survive a lion attack only to die in a hospital?

XXIII

He and the donkey climbed the escarpment, taking their time. Aside from baboons grazing in the brush beside the trail, they were alone. They followed a path, doubtless formed by pastoralists toggling between pastures on the slopes and the spring below, but met neither flocks nor herders. The air was still, unusually so, perhaps for the shelter of the slope, and besides his own and Dapple's steps and their breathing he could hear bird calls and nothing else. He was unsure where he was going, except up. For now he was simply following somebody else's path, placing one foot in front of the other, waiting for what would present itself. He was not entirely without will. He did not want to be more than two or three hours from the spring, which was the only water supply he knew. He had no intention of going all the way to the top, where he would meet the continental highway, which extended north to the other capital and followed the rim far to the east before dropping south and linking this country with the one he'd left behind. He had no interest in reaching that road. His one intention, if you could call it that, was to be lost, bide his time, be a mountain hermit, see how that felt. Whatever came after could wait.

The path was steep. He was breathing hard but was not winded.

Dapple moved steadily in front so he could keep up and did not need to pause to catch his breath. He kept his eyes on the gullied clay and stones at his feet, following the switchbacks as they turned, rarely looking up for the view.

He thought of nothing in particular but always it was himself. Not dead on, not so he was aware of it, or if asked so he'd admit it. But obliquely, surreptitiously, as if he was catching his eye in the mirror of a public place. It was always himself that held his attention: likes and dislikes, things he noticed or ignored, what pleased or annoyed, pleasures of long ago, hazards of the night before. Of the baboons, for instance, at the spring below, he wondered how they spent the night, fireless and fearful. Even thoughts of them turned back on himself. Had they survived what he managed to escape? How did their fear compare to his own?

He thought of his growing hunger, of the dusty emptiness in his belly since a breakfast of rice and stewed leftovers from the night before, the weakness in his knees. He wondered what he would eat when his provisions ran out. He had rice, potatoes, onions, sugar, and tea leaves to last a week or two. It was a meager diet. For water he would drop to the spring. For food, however, he'd have to trek all the way back to Forole. Or climb the rest of the way up. Mega, a town on the road, would not be more than a day's hard walk away, but he wasn't sure which was closer, Forole or Mega. There would be more food options at Mega than Forole. He'd have to be careful, though, think through what time of day he was least likely to attract the attention of police or soldiers or whatever they had there. He'd driven through Mega once and remembered it being impossible to enter without being noticed by virtually everyone. On that point he supposed there was an advantage to being a foreigner. Yes, he was conspicuous, but so was any stranger in a small town. His conspicuousness, however, came with a tincture of power, for *ferenji* like him wielded influence, even here, and were not harassed for fear of consequences. Only a very confident soldier would challenge him. He thought. He hoped. The worst, he thought, would be like Duba at Badda Hurri: throwing their weight around, reminding him of their power, such as it was, and in the end letting him go. But he was naïve about these matters. He simply didn't know.

His mind drifted from one thought to another, one threat to another. Always the threat reminded him of the threat he posed and exercised, the power he had held over her, the power of desire, he supposed, pulling her into his world without much regard for her, then stumbling onward to the threat she'd posed to him, and for what reason. How could she, how dare she? His mind followed the switchbacks, turning here and again there: A loosened rock, nicked by a hoof, falling the ten feet back to where he trod and sidestepped it, caught his attention and changed his direction, and he wandered off in another. Once he saw the tail of a cobra—what must have been a cobra judging from its length—disappear into the brush beside the trail. If he were hunting spirits, there were plenty to be found. Each intruding, each leaving as quickly. He was lost to himself, buffeted by thought upon thought, in their charge, not his own. Walking, notions flitting here and there like birds in a desert bush, one rumination after another.

The bleat of a lamb startled him to attention. Where there were sheep were people, and he didn't want to see people.

The path climbed onto a wide ledge, a plateau of sorts, partway up the escarpment. He could see the path winding below. He wasn't sure where it led from here up. Near the path were two tents and near them was a small flock of white lambs tended by a child, who paused and stared at him, then ran to one of the tents and disappeared inside. There followed a couple of beats and then a woman's head looked out from the tent, from between the flaps of cloth that served as a door, and then her head disappeared. He was the last thing anybody here expected to climb up from the spring below. An old man came out of the other tent and stood, and he stood and greeted the old man in the way of old man greetings.

Bultisan nagaya?

Nagaa, kesan nagaa, the old man answered.

Horisan nagaya?

Nagaa, nagaa.

Ijole urgoftu?

Urgoftu.

The old man smiled.

The greetings went on for several minutes, giving each time to assess the other, communicating little more than lack of ill will. He leaned on the spear he'd been carrying, making it a walking staff, planting his right leg behind his left leg, glad to have arrived somewhere, calculating that this was a good spot to camp except for the camp already here.

It was a small *olla* of two Dasse tents, occupied by an old couple in one and their son, his wife, and their few children in the other. There was also a collection of large *kara*, rock shelters for the kids and lambs, and a tall stone corral for sheep and goats. These were fortresses. He thought of the lion last night.

He was curious to find such a small family by itself, alone like this. The old man explained that his son worked for a Bible translator at Mega.

He knew of Catholic priests scattered across the wider region with interests and knowledge in local languages and culture. He also knew Protestant missionaries, mostly isolated families working for any number of small church organizations, who settled in places like Mega and learned the local languages. They spent years working on Biblical and liturgical translations, often with the help of young men such as the old man's son, men with a little schooling. It could have been Protestants or Catholics at Mega. He no longer knew, was out of touch with church activities. The family was camped here to be near the son, so they could visit. They were a poor family, without camels, that much was obvious, and this was what they could manage: tending their sheep and goats on the slopes, fetching water in jerry cans on their backs from below. They must have borrowed a few camels to move themselves here and, next time they moved, would have to borrow camels again. It was a hard life. But the son was making money, and though it couldn't be much, he thought that it was on him that the family was building its hopes. Still it seemed strange for them to have isolated themselves this way from the rest of a community.

It was also strange that the old man did not invite him to sit, to have tea.

The little boy who had disappeared into the one tent re-emerged and now stood holding the old man's leg, staring unabashedly, casting a look now and then to the lambs that skittered below the bushes nearby. Dapple browsed, content for the time being not to be climbing. Neither woman had come out of her tent. He assumed they were both inside listening, perhaps afraid.

The old man asked him where he was from.

He said the name of his country but could see that meant little to the old man, so he told him he'd been staying at Toricha, that he'd left and gone to Badda Hurri, then Forole, and now here. The old man asked for news of Badda Hurri. He told the old man about Ado's mother, that she was ill. He did not tell him about the Ayana rite, for the old man might have misunderstood. He said he didn't know anyone else at Badda Hurri and didn't have any other news. He told him Chief Boru was away from Forole, that people there had said Boru had gone to Marsabit.

The old man asked where he was going and what he was looking for.

Maan barabad? he said.

Imbeku, he said. I don't know.

Then he added, because not knowing was ridiculous, that he was looking around for pasture and a good place to camp. This was a generic but acceptable answer for a pastoralist. It was the sort of thing Dasse men said when they were, in fact, as he was, looking for a place to camp.

The old man said there was not much good pasture here, that the life was not so good, but it was not bad either; the land supported his few goats and sheep, and they were all healthy.

The old man asked if he had animals.

He answered that there was just the donkey, which puzzled the old man, who was too polite to question him further.

He presented the old man with a dilemma. Good manners required the man to invite the stranger to stay, despite their meager resources. But he was anxious about a stranger who didn't seem to have proper aims or means for livelihood: Why would a poor man without animals seek pasture?

He asked how far the flat shelf they stood on extended, and the old man said it went very far to the west. He asked if there were other camps that way. The old man said there was none. The *ferenji* decided to go west, look for a place to camp, and perhaps make camp there, not near, but not far—over that way. He was vague. What could the old man say? He imagined the old man was even more perplexed by someone preferring to be alone, not asking to camp with them or nearby.

There wasn't much basis for either to be comfortable with the other: Neither wanted the other's company, and that fact itself aroused their mutual suspicions. Only bandits and witches avoided the company of others.

The old man said there was no milk for tea.

He lifted and waved an open hand to reassure the man and said, *Yaqufa, anan qufa.*

The man's face relaxed, but his eyes continued to question the presence of the stranger, who answered him by saying, *nagayat*, stay in peace, then clicked his tongue for the donkey and departed.

❖

Have made camp two miles west of a small olla *occupied by old man and family. Two tents. Awkward. They didn't want me around but could not say it. I didn't want them. What could we do? I had no language to tell them why I wanted to be alone, and they had no cultural understanding to make sense of this, except to know that such behavior was suspicious. Nothing wrong with traveling alone, but with them the destination is always social. How queer to aim for solitude. Maybe I should have told them I have* hamtu, *or was outcast. It makes sense they would want to be close to a son, who apparently works at Mega, but to be just these two tents on a hillside is also strange: It suggests if nothing else that they are not well connected, certainly not well heeled.*

❖

Have found a flat space in the shade of a wide acacia overlooking plains to the south and west. Good views. Good place to sit and think. I cannot see Marsabit or Maikona. Perhaps that's best. I can see parts of Badda Hurri, which look from here like a jumble of rounded shark's teeth biting into an otherwise flat plain, or old tombstones punctuating a graveyard. Cloudless skies. Absolutely clear. I can hear wind above and below but, protected by the slope, the wind here is not so bad.

❖

I've begun to build a stone shelter, the sort of thing Dasse build for lambs, only bigger, a rock igloo. There are plenty of rocks. I cleared a wide smooth yard, maybe twenty-five or thirty feet across. In the midst of this I laid a circle of large stones, seven or eight feet across, and began stacking more rocks on top. The circle is slowly becoming a wall. There's no mortar, and I am no engineer. There'll be no space for Dapple. The donkey will have to be content with the thorn-branch corral I made first, for the both of us. I have no idea what I am doing, but I am learning quickly and have fallen into a rhythm: finding suitable rocks, large and flat, setting them upon the rim of rocks, settling them into some sort of stable configuration, finding more rocks. I can carry one big one or three smaller ones: one in the crook of my left arm, the other two in my hands.

⁂

After several hours of carrying rocks I enlisted Dapple. I saddled him without the jerry cans and place large rocks in the cradle on either side. Still have to walk back and forth but don't get so tired carrying the rocks myself.

⁂

The old man showed up. He greeted, stood at a distance, and watched. He smiled. After a couple of rock-carrying trips the old man drew closer and then began to help arrange the stones, tentatively at first but soon he was in charge, correcting my placements, then he was placing rocks and I was fetching them. After an hour or so he asked where I would sleep. He assumed the corral was for Dapple. It isn't big enough for the both of us. He shook his head and laughed when I told him it was for me. Dapple would stay in the thorn corral. He warned about lions, said I should build a stone corral for the donkey as well. That'll require more rocks.

⁂

My plan was to build a stone shelter, including a roof, a dome of stones, like the little shelters for kids and lambs. The old man told me that is not possible. There is no way to keep the stones over my head. They'll fall down and bury me. He thought it was funny I was so ignorant about building a shelter. I told him I worried that a lion could leap over the wall. He said that was possible. He asked if I had a cloth tent—I suppose he meant canvas—that I could spread across the top. He said he had seen soldiers with cloth tents, canvas tarps from the sound of it, which they stretched across stones for shelter. I said I did not have a tent. He nodded. I fetched rocks. He placed them. The wall grows taller.

⁂

The old man brought an ostrich egg today. It's a beautiful object, heavy, round, size of a skull, yellowish, color of old ivory or bone, smooth as a river rock. You'd have liked the color, the smooth weathered look, despite its being so fresh and new. I wondered aloud what I should do with it. He was amused I had to ask. Eat it, he said. Indeed. I could use a change of diet. Dasse don't eat eggs, or birds, or anything that doesn't look like a goat or sheep or cow or camel. They'll eat giraffe. They'll eat buffalo. But they won't eat zebra. And they certainly won't eat ostrich or its eggs. The old man, I realized, is not Dasse but Waata, a hunter-gatherer. I assumed he was Dasse.

Like all the Waata I know, his language is Dasse, his dress is Dasse, he sleeps in a Dasse tent, takes care of Dasse animals. I knew this about Waata. Lots of Dasse camps have Waata living with them. As far as I know Waata have lost their own language. I've never heard them speak it, anyway. The big difference is they'll eat things Dasse won't eat, like ostrich eggs. Dasse regard Waata as sacred people, autochthonous, the original people of the place. They also think Waata make poor pastoralists. It's like Waata are Dasse and not Dasse at the same time. Dasse dislike Waata. But they also seek their blessings and avoid their curses. It's a good thing the Waata man has taken an interest in me. He's really helped with the wall.

⁂

I figured out the roof. It was the old man's suggestion that I lay canvas across the stones. That reminded me of the hos, *the shelter for the* d'abella *at* sorio hamtu. *So this morning I dug a hole in the center of the corral. Then I found a tree, not a big one, just about nine or ten feet tall. The trunk was about six inches in diameter and took me most of the morning to cut with my panga, which is just a big knife. Almost gave up a couple of times. I couldn't lift the tree by myself, but the old man came and helped and we carried it to the wall and planted it inside. I used rocks to keep it plumb, filled the rest of the hole with dirt, and tamped it firm. Then I cut branches like for the corral and laid them between the wall and the branches of the tree. The thorns in the treetop and the thorns in the branches clasp together. It's amazingly secure. Now I've got a house with a roof made of tree branches and a wall made of rocks. It won't keep out rain, not that I have to worry much about that, but it just might keep out a lion. It took three days.*

XXIV

Watching the fire that night in front of the shelter, he thought of the many ways there were to get stuck. You could get stuck in mud. You could get stuck in sand. You could get stuck in snow. You could get stuck with a flat tire. You could get stuck in a job. You could get stuck with a knife. You could get stuck with the bill. You could get stuck thinking about getting stuck. And getting stuck wasn't just staying put. You could get stuck in repetition, doing something over and over, a skip in a vinyl record, a swirl of indecision.

Once, early on, they'd vacationed in mountains, rented a couple of kayaks, and paddled a white river. It was the first excursion, the first journey. But it had stuck them on a path together that led to one place and then another, to Maikona and Marsabit and eventually to that hospice bed in the back room. And while that first trip influenced the character and direction of the subsequent journey, it determined nothing. It simply set in motion a series of causes and consequences. And it had its own antecedents. Prior events interfered. There was never a truly first mark on canvas, no mover unmoved, no original state. This was his belated insight. One responded to what was already there. There was *always* something already there. In that way responsibility was shared. One couldn't avoid it. The opposite, in fact. He was always in over his head.

⁂

They'd rented two boats, paddles, and wet gear from an outfitter near the river. They each had some experience, which they exaggerated to get the kayaks. They'd manage. The river was low. They could always stop, carry the boats around a tricky part. They paid the deposit. They locked cameras, clothes, and wallets in the car. The man at the counter, a stoner with a black T-shirt and grizzled beard, handed each a map of the river, a cartoon actually, like a map of an amusement park, which depicted rapids with names such as Table Saw, Spin Cycle, Double Suck, and Pincher. It was water. They were swimmers, fit, young. Life was an adventure. How hard could it be?

A school bus carried the boats on its roof along with a fleet of rubber rafts for other renters. At the put-in, they carried the boats to the shoreline. The kayaks reminded him of plastic kazoos. His was red, hers green. They tied their gear inside. They slithered into the hatch, feet first, like squeezing into a tight pair of jeans, fixed the skirts on the cockpit lips, and pushed off. Their pointy noses kissed. He flicked cold water at her with the paddle. She returned the favor. They laughed. They let the rafters go ahead so they could take their time, be alone. They pulled into the sun-dazzled current. The water, clean out of a national forest, rolled over amber-colored rocks, but where it was deep, the water was dark.

They spent the morning drifting through calm sections that lay between surprisingly easy rapids. The rapids for the most part consisted of a narrowing river, a quickening pace, a concentration of water and waves down the middle, a bend in front of a boulder, a drop into a pool. His confidence rose. Neither had spilled. They took turns going first, slipping into an eddy below to watch the other follow. There was laughter and hooting. Mountains rose steeply on both sides. Towering hemlocks stood beside the river. Roots, like the claws of dinosaurs, clung to the banks, as if the trees were waiting to pounce.

They lunched on a flat rock in a bend that the map called Lunch Stop. They swam in the pool below and lay in the sun to dry. She'd brought a pad and pencils in her dry bag and pulled these out and sketched the opposite bank. After a nap he noticed a front of dark clouds, thunderheads, far to the north. But the wind was blowing from the west, the sky warm and clear, the storm a long way off. He didn't mention the clouds. He didn't want them getting in the way.

You're a natural, he said.

Thanks to all those summers in camp.

The water suits you.

I could do this forever, she said. Let's be river guides.

We'd be bored in a week.

Not me.

Sure you would. The same river, day after day?

Shut up! She laughed and threw one of the wet towels at his face. Let me have a fantasy. I can pretend, can't I?

OK, river guide. Lead on.

He knew it wasn't the river that would have bored her. She'd have found the subtle variations of light on water endlessly fascinating. It was being with all the people that would have worn her out.

They meandered south. The rapids grew more complicated.

In the pillow formed by water rushing over a round boulder, he lost his balance, rolled, and spilled out of the boat. He floated feet first into calmer water. He'd held his paddle but lost the boat, which she retrieved and towed to shore. He emptied out the water while she waited, and they shoved off. Nothing much to worry about. But there was more water now than that morning. He was sure of it. The rapids were more forceful and insistent. He couldn't remember passing any streams flowing into the river that would explain the rise. They paid less attention to each other, more to the river.

The next rapid, rated intermediate to advanced on the map, depending on water level, was called *Jail.* It involved two consecutive bends best executed with an eddy turn after the first, a ferry across to the other side so you would approach the second curve away from an overhang, and then a hard push across the final drop. There was a nasty hole at the drop that, at high water levels, created a churn of backflow that paddlers called a *keeper*. Hence the section's name.

The guy at the counter thought the river level was low enough that they'd shoot through without a problem.

He wondered whether the guy had factored in whatever was causing the river to rise.

He went first and, despite initial jitters, managed the eddy turn and ferry. When he saw the drop and heard its roar, he knew he'd have to dig to punch through the roiling water below. As it turned out, his paddle caught the last bit of solid water before the fall, and he just managed to shove himself past. He felt a shudder in the tail, which he thought must have been the hydraulic trying to hold on. He turned in the pool below to warn her, but because of the bends in the river he couldn't see her. He shouted, though he knew she wouldn't hear. The water was thunderous. The water was more yellow than white. The sky, incongruously clear.

He saw the green boat before he saw her and saw at once there was a problem. Something had happened in one of the bends. She was approaching the drop in reverse, unable to get a good view, unlikely to make a sufficient dig to clear the hydraulic. The kayak fell over the drop, and she lost her balance and tipped. Somehow she managed to roll the boat right. She was still in trouble. Hard paddling inched her forward but the keeper pulled her back against the ledge. Water was flowing over the deck fore and aft. She was trapped in the froth.

He drove his boat to shore and jerked himself out, scraping the side of one knee. Later he saw his calf was covered in blood. At the time he didn't notice. He stood on a rock prepared to do something. But what? He had no rope. His paddle wasn't long enough to reach.

Meanwhile, she was exhausting herself trying to pull free.

Reach beyond the foam! he shouted.

She looked at him but didn't hear.

Her face was puzzled, worried.

Again she looked to him and back at the water. She paddled furiously. She would tire. She needed help. And he could do nothing. Jumping in and swimming to her would be foolish. He'd only make matters worse and become entrapped himself.

She knew to reach her paddle into relatively still water. He could see her trying. The problem was the white water held so much air and movement that it offered little purchase. Each time she leaned to reach she risked capsizing again.

And then she did.

All of a sudden there was just the bottom of her boat. He could see it rock as she tried to right it, and then it was flotsam, a plastic bottle bobbing in the foam.

Her head popped to the surface.

She looked at him once more and not again. Even with the life vest, she was having to work hard to stay afloat. She was working to breathe. She was no longer trying to escape. She was holding up. She was not looking at him.

Do something! he screamed.

He screamed to himself. She couldn't hear.

All he could do was watch and feel ashamed for not having the foresight to bring a rope to throw. He wanted only to make contact, to reach her. It occurred to him to throw a stick, a log, even a rock, anything to make contact, to do something, cross the distance. Of course it was madness. It was the madness of uncertainty, the madness of paralysis.

Now she was moving.

She removed her helmet and tossed it aside.

She hadn't had her paddle since she escaped the boat.

She unbuckled the life vest.

What was she thinking?

No! he shouted.

She did not look at him.

She let herself sink into the water.

No! he shouted. What are you doing?

But she was gone.

He stared at the churning water.

The rapids changed. Everything went still. The water didn't freeze; it simply stopped. Where before the foam had been milky, there were now individual bubbles. He might have counted them. The water was liquid. It poured over the rocks. It was still wet. But it wasn't moving anymore. He saw the water. He saw into the water. He saw the stone ledge that formed the drop, the yellow and gray beneath falling water that was still falling but no longer in motion. The sound melted away.

He prayed to the rock. He prayed to the water. He prayed to the air.

They were all that was left.

He didn't even know he was praying.

He prayed despite himself.

He was unbelieving. Unbelieving what she'd done. Unbelieving what he hoped or prayed would make a difference.

He turned in search of someone, anyone, who could lend a hand or offer advice or simply witness his helplessness. He wanted to jump after her and he wanted to live, and he thought the former impulse was wrong and he thought the latter was wrong, and his inability to help and his unwillingness to do the one heroic stupid thing he could think to do made him feel sick and ashamed.

And then, beside a standing boulder below the boil, her head rose from out of the water.

Her head was up, coughing, face forward, eyes wide, bewildered, frightened, alive.

The roar of the rapid returned.

He plunged to her.

They clasped.

You just stood there, she said, sobbing, gasping for air.

There was nothing to say. He held her and wept.

I know, she said. I know.

She'd done the one thing left to her. She'd sunk into the boil, dived to the bottom, found rocks to hold, and pulled herself away from the suck into the dark cold waters beyond, and then swum to the surface and air.

And, much as he thought now, before the fire, that he'd made it his life's habit of doing, he stood by and witnessed and watched and did nothing.

What could he do? He'd been stuck on that question as long as he knew.

XXV

He fell into a new routine. He woke early, pissed and shat in the bush at some far distance from camp, rekindled the fire, made tea, reheated whatever he'd had for supper the night before, cleaned up, sat, watched. One day, soon after he'd finished the shelter and an adjacent stone corral for Dapple, he and the donkey walked back to the spring, where they met about a dozen herders and more than a hundred camels. He visited with them, refilled the jerry cans, and returned to camp. Otherwise he sat in front of the shelter and watched the plains below, writing in the journal, listening, smelling, breathing. He did, in fact, very little. It was enough to sit and watch. His writing more and more focused simply on what he saw, such as the sky at sunset, telling his wife, the painter, not to inform her but so she'd know he noticed: *glow of new fire on old snow, rose petals fallen on oak floor, india ink spilled on blotter paper*. Then nouns: animals, insects, plants, configurations of soil and rock, shadows, and shadows within shadows. Eventually he gave up words altogether and drew, sketching the horizon line, the curve of a branch, the shape of his hut, Dapple's tail, his calloused and dirty feet at the end of his legs, his sandals, a moth killed by the evening fire, the fire itself. He remembered the painter's description of her own method: You make one mark, then another—it makes a pattern. He was doing that now. One mark, then another.

The old man sometimes visited late in the afternoon. He sensed the man was checking on him, making sure he was OK, out of some basic human sense of responsibility. The old man couldn't have had much confidence in the other's abilities to survive on his own. Perhaps this reassured the old man's fears. Each day he visited: There was the stranger, still alive, just sitting, alone. Strange. They talked little.

The old man asked for news: *Daemptu maan?*

His answer was always the same.

Nagaya challa. Only peace.

⁂

You came last night. Or did you? I'd fallen asleep. The donkey woke me. I heard it through the stones. It was stomping the ground and snorting, clearly agitated. I thought lion, and my heart leaped into my mouth. The fire outside had gone to embers so I went out and added wood. The flames rose bright and yellow, expanding the ring of light. It lit up the entire underside of the tree where I have made my home. Then you stepped into the edge of the light. I knew it was not you, that you were not really there, but I also knew that it was you, completely, that this was all you were, all you'd ever been. You wore the trousers and paint-stained shirt you used to wear in your studio. You were barefoot. I noticed that. I thought of the thorns. You walked into the light and stood. You did not call. You did not smile. You looked my way, but I could not say for certain that you looked at me, though you might have. You looked toward me and Dapple and the fire. I did not call either, caught as I was in the uncertainty, knowing you were not there, knowing you were, knowing the beauty was real, and not wanting to ruin it with my voice.

⁂

Late one afternoon, as the sun fell below the far horizon and he began to think of building the evening fire, a cobra crawled into the dust in front of the shelter. It slid over to him and lifted itself, eyes level with his. He was afraid but also intrigued. He had never encountered a snake like this before, a snake with curiosity. The snake swayed side to side and he swayed with it. They danced like this. Was it the snake or he that led? He could not be sure. They swayed together.

Before he was aware the snake's mouth opened, and he saw the hurl of spit, the venom, tongue-like, and then he saw nothing, and then he felt what could only have been the snake's face hit his own face, like a fist, a slap, a burning iron on his cheek. The panic of sightlessness, the sting of a bite, his face exploding in pain, simply from the idea of what had happened. Was the snake not a dream?

Later he woke, sitting where he had been sitting, hunched over, sleep drool hanging to his hands. When he rose he found the track of a snake, like a bike's tires, crossing in the dust in front of the house.

⁂

There is another night. He is relaxed, in a way he has not experienced in weeks, since coming, in a way that has been dawning all day. Peace. Contentment. They were just words. Perhaps at last he has found a place, a hermitage, that suits him. The old challenges are wearing off. The old man did not visit that afternoon. He has made and eaten a supper of rice and potatoes, some bits of meat the old man shared the day before. The onions are finished. He is going to have to make a journey for more food. Despite these circumstances, he is aware of his contentment, an ease of breath, absence of worry, attention to the present. He finishes early, cleans his two small pots, his dish and spoon. He leads Dapple into the stone corral that stands beside and shares part of a wall with his own shelter. He makes the night fire, outside, which he builds now more for the comfort of light than the protection it offers. The last few nights he has even let the fire die of its own, not bothering to feed it and keep it alive. The fire is company, warm, animate, reminding him of other, more cheerful fires, happier times, and this is why he builds it. He looks over the journal, the sketches he made that afternoon, and while he is not pleased with them—they are nothing he would show anyone but her—he considers them done and shown, that she is somehow privy to the task he has set, which is to make marks, tracing the lines that he sees, giving them shape and shadow, documenting them, endowing them with a sort of life: one mark, then another. The practice fills his day, occupies the gaps between basic chores of survival, fetching water, cooking, seeing to Dapple's needs.

Eventually he closes the book, spits out the now flavorless tobacco he's chewed since supper, ducks into his hut beneath the tree, the trees: the smaller one inside that is his shelter and the larger one outside that shades the other. He lies down on the skin. His bed is to the left as he enters, in the rear, the place for the husband of the house. He smiles at this thought, this ethnographic detail. He wonders if she is over on the right, whether this is where she lies, would lie, if she were here. He shakes the thought away and tries not to think of her, tries not to think of anything. He looks up through the branches of the two trees, the inner one and the outer one, and sees a few stars that are not eclipsed by the branches. He closes his eyes and falls asleep.

Dapple wakes him. Dapple is disturbed by something. This has happened on other nights and nothing has come of it. He rises anyway, clucks soothingly to the donkey, adds a couple of pieces of wood to the dying fire, builds it back again. The donkey, however, remains addled, snorts, stomps the ground. He sits by the fire and keeps vigil for a few minutes. Dapple eventually quiets down. He feeds the fire again, then withdraws to his bed.

He has no idea how long it has been, no idea of the time, but there is still some dim light from the fire outside and Dapple is wailing through the stones beside his head. He jumps up, alarmed, grabs his electric torch and, as he emerges from the hut, picks up the spear leaning beside the doorway. At just this moment Dapple loses all sense of safety in the corral and tries to leap the wall, which is much too high in too tight of a space to clear, and the wall tumbles beneath his weight. Dapple stumbles, kicks at the air, and bucks toward the edge of the firelight.

Only then does he notice the lion, which has been waiting for this and now takes two seemingly effortless bounds toward the donkey. Dapple, screaming, kicks both rear legs at the lion, which recoils, ears back, hissing.

He doesn't hear the hiss. He sees it. And now he doesn't think. He drops the torch and lifts the spear high above his head and runs at the lion, an athlete, a spear thrower, running as fast as he can in the five or six steps that it takes, shouting as loudly and as long as his one last breath allows. He shoves the spear at the beast but knows in the instant that the spear will do no good. He is not practiced. Has never practiced. Knows next to nothing of spears, even less of killing a lion, where even to aim on its body. He thrusts as hard as he can. And though he knows so little he knows that it is not enough. He hits the beast but in no essential place, and the lion is so much larger, weighs so much more, has so much more practice and less hesitation than he.

Aérogramme

Dear ______,

Eleven weeks ago, Elema Guyo, Abudo's surviving brother, visited Father Roba at Maikona with the story that you were killed by a lion across the border. Elema wondered if it was true. Roba sent news of Elema's report to me, and I sent instructions back that he should ask Elema to investigate. By that time, of course, Elema was off somewhere with his camels, and Roba had no idea how to reach him. What was I thinking?

The boy Ali was enlisted. He retraced your route to Forole, where he met an old man who said you had camped near him on the escarpment. The man said that one day he found your camp in ruins. He discovered the carcass of the donkey in the bush, what was left of it. He also found the tracks of a single lion. There was no sign of you, however, and no indication of what might have happened to you. No clothes, no food, no cooking equipment, no water containers, no rucksack. The old man said he saw footprints of other men. He feared bandits might have captured you or herd boys might have taken your things. This is what he told Ali.

Ali found your camp. He confirmed the man's story: he discovered the bones of the donkey, the tumbled-down corral. Ali found something the others missed: on a ledge inside the shelter was a notebook that he recognized as yours. In it are writings and drawings. Ali carried the notebook back to Maikona, and from there it was sent to me via Abdullah's lorry. I shall keep the notebook until I hear from you.

The people of Forole think you were carried off by the lion. I can't believe it. So I write in hopes of an answer.

I pray for your wife, God bless her soul, whose good work is remembered in Marsabit.

You will be glad to hear the rains have come. They are never enough, but for now everything will be all right. Well, not everything. But the animals are happy.

Yours truly, in God's name,

Father ______, North Horr, Marsabit District

From an article in *The Journal of the Royal Anthropological Institute* (formerly known as *Man*):

...Dasse tell a story about a white man and woman from far away who once came and traveled with them. The couple had no children. They had no animals. They had no property. They were wanderers, probably witches. Witches or spirits. The woman could not bear to be seen and wore a veil. She drew pictures, even on rocks, even in the dirt. The man sat with the men and asked questions. Elders were unsure at first what to tell him and what to keep secret. But the white man asked questions of little consequence, so they told him what he wanted to know. What did it matter? The couple was seen walking together among the stones. They had no animals. It was as though they were following animals, but they did not have animals. They climbed hills, looked over the land. Eventually they went away. No one knows just where, but young people said it was to the south. They left one day and did not return. Years later the man came back alone. Once again he traveled with Dasse, though this time he asked no questions. He did not stay long. He was a nomad without animals. He wandered off alone into the bush. There it is said he was eaten

by a lion. Some people deny this and say he went mad and became a lion himself. Whatever actually happened, he was never seen again, though some believe he wanders among them at night, listening to camp sounds, disturbing the animals. He is a story parents tell children to frighten them. Anthropologists who visit Dasse and hear the story ask what it means. Elders shrug and say it is just a story. It has no meaning...

Acknowledgments

A book, like a person, owes much to many. Time for the fieldwork and writing of this book was made possible over the years by the Wenner-Gren Foundation, the National Geographic Society, the Max Planck Institute for Social Anthropology, Emory University, the University of Nairobi, and the University of North Carolina at Asheville. The following family, friends, and colleagues read, commented, and dispensed wisdom: Ken Betsalel, Mindy Clark, David Colman, Tim Colman, Robert Cumming, Henry Dommann, Volker Frank, Yara Golo, Bill Haas, Abudo Halake, Tommy Hays, Judy Hoffman, Heidi Kelley, Melvin Konner, Daniel Lende, Joel and Claudia Leonard, Liam Luttrell-Rowland, Jared and Alice Massanari, Sebastian Matthews, Katherine Min, Midge Raymond, Cynthia Salvadori, David Schenck, Rosa Shand, Father Paul Tablino, Ken and Sauni Wood, Lindy Wood, Peter Wood, and John Yunker. Many others too numerous to list supported and encouraged. To all, thank you. I managed to accomplish the shortcomings on my own. I am especially indebted to Gabra pastoralists of the Chalbi region of northern Kenya and southern Ethiopia. They sometimes refer to themselves as Wara Dasse, people of matted tents, a name I have borrowed. It is Gabra funerary customs that are described throughout. The rest is story. The book is dedicated to Carol Young Wood, whose patience, generosity, and intelligence comprise the without-which-nothing.

About the Author

Photo credit: Carol Young Wood

John Colman Wood teaches at the University of North Carolina at Asheville. He has been doing fieldwork with Gabra nomads in northern Kenya and southern Ethiopia on and off since 1991. His fiction has appeared in *Anthropology and Humanism*, and he has twice won the Ethnographic Fiction Prize of the Society for Humanistic Anthropology, once for a story extracted from *The Names of Things*. He is also the author of *When Men Are Women: Manhood among Gabra Nomads of East Africa* (University of Wisconsin Press). Before becoming an anthropologist, Wood was a journalist.

Ashland Creek Press is a small, independent publisher of books with a world view. From travel narratives to eco-literature, our mission is to publish a range of books that foster an appreciation for worlds outside our own, for nature and the animal kingdom, and for the ways in which we all connect. To keep up-to-date on new and forthcoming works, subscribe to our free newsletter by visiting: www.AshlandCreekPress.com.

CPSIA information can be obtained at www.ICGtesting.com
Printed in the USA
BVOW07s0626040913

330078BV00001B/2/P